TH**EY** **BEHAVED** LI**KE** **SOLDIERS**

Captain John Chilton
and the
Third Virginia Regiment

1775-1778

Michael Cecere

HERITAGE BOOKS
2004

HERITAGE BOOKS
AN IMPRINT OF HERITAGE BOOKS, INC.

Books, CDs, and more – Worldwide

For our listing of thousands of titles see our website
at
www.HeritageBooks.com

Published 2004 by
HERITAGE BOOKS, INC.
Publishing Division
1540 Pointer Ridge Place #E
Bowie, Maryland 20716

International Standard Book Number: 0-7884-2479-3

Contents

Maps

Acknowledgements

I want to thank my wife, Susan, and our children, Jenny and Michael, for tolerating my obsession with the American Revolution. Fellow teacher Marguerite Knickmeyer and fellow re-enactor David McKissack deserve my thanks as well, for their valuable writing advice and encouragement. I also want to thank the Revolutionary War reenacting community for providing numerous opportunities, and a positive environment in which to learn more about this era. The interest and commitment of my fellow re-enactors is inspiring. Lastly, I want to thank my students, who, from time to time asked me how my book was coming. That simple question made me realize that if my students believed I could write a book, perhaps I really could.

Dedicated to my grandparents,

Bruno and Rita Mazzeo,

whose support, and stories,

helped foster my love of history.

Introduction

At first glance, there is little about Captain John Chilton's Revolutionary War record that makes him more memorable than the thousands of other soldiers who fought for America's independence. His military experiences, the marches, battles, hardships and frustrations, were ones that many soldiers shared. Yet, thanks to the survival of Chilton's letters and diary, we have access to his detailed observations, thoughts and emotions.

We see a man who was deeply concerned about the well-being of his family. Chilton's letters are full of inquiries and instructions for his children. His letters also express pride and concern for the men in his company.

These men were members of the 3rd Virginia Regiment, the first unit of Virginia regulars to join General Washington's army in New York. They served, with distinction, at Harlem Heights, Trenton, Morristown, Brandywine, Germantown, and Valley Forge.

Yet, it is not the battles that Chilton offers insight into, but rather, the more routine aspects of life in the American army. The struggles in camp and on the march, the encounters with fellow officers and local inhabitants, the hopes and expectations of Chilton and his men, these are the aspects highlighted by Chilton's letters and diary. And these are the things that make the story of John Chilton, and the 3rd Virginia Regiment, so interesting and memorable.

Chapter One

"Our Business was to Counteract Dunmore"

Gunpowder Incident

British troops quietly entered Williamsburg in the early morning hours of April 21st, 1775. Lord Dunmore, the Royal Governor of Virginia, had given them a simple mission. They were to transfer the colony's gunpowder from the powder magazine, in the middle of town, to a British ship anchored four miles away in the James River.[1] Dunmore hoped that this would end the growing talk of armed resistance to British policies.[2]

When the seizure was discovered, however, it did just the opposite, igniting a firestorm of anger and protest that swept the colony. Outraged townspeople in Williamsburg threatened to storm the Governor's Palace, and independent militia companies throughout Virginia prepared to march on the capital. Reports that British troops had conducted similar raids in Massachusetts and North Carolina only confirmed the view of many Virginians, that Dunmore's actions were part of a plot to disarm and coerce all of the colonies.[3]

Surprised and concerned at the extent of public outrage, Lord Dunmore tried to defuse the crisis by agreeing to pay for the seized gunpowder. Although this succeeded in easing tensions a bit, relations between the Governor and the

---

[1] John E. Selby, <u>The Revolution in Virginia : 1775-1783</u>, (New York : Holt Inc., 1996), 2

[2] Ibid.

[3] Ibid. 3

colonists were irreparably damaged. The situation remained volatile through May, culminating on June 8th, with Dunmore and his family fleeing Williamsburg for the safety of a British ship.[4] He immediately began organizing a military force to reassert his royal authority. He looked to Britain for help, but with London's attention focused on Massachusetts, little help was forthcoming. A call for loyal Virginians to take up arms and support the crown was disappointing. By autumn, Dunmore resorted to granting freedom to slaves in return for their service.[5] Even this, however, produced only a few hundred, poorly trained soldiers.

No such manpower shortage faced the 3rd Virginia Convention, the new, de facto government of the colony. Convention delegates met in August to fill the power vacuum created by Governor Dunmore's departure. They formed a temporary government and a new military establishment for the colony. The independent militia companies that had formed themselves in 1774-75 were replaced by a new, three-tiered military system. The top tier consisted of two, 500 man units, designated the 1st and 2nd Virginia Battalions. These full-time, "regular" soldiers were raised throughout the colony and served for one year.[6] Such a force had not been raised in Virginia since the war with France twenty years earlier.

The next tier consisted of fifteen battalions of Minutemen. The men selected for these units were better trained and prepared than their counter-parts in the last tier, the regular militia. Every free white male between the ages of 16 and 50 belonged to the militia, but only those who were fit and able to serve at a moment's notice were selected for the minute companies.[7]

---

[4] Ibid. 43
[5] Ibid. 66
[6] William Hening, <u>The Statutes at Large being a collection of all the Laws of Virginia from the first session of the Legislature, Vol. 9,</u> (1821), 10
[7] Selby, 52

Enlistment in both the regular and minute battalions was strong and soldiers streamed into Williamsburg, eager for a confrontation with Lord Dunmore. He continued to have problems raising his own military force, however, and stayed safely onboard ships lying off Hampton.

By autumn, the residents of Williamsburg had grown quite accustomed to armed men around town. Yet, the arrival of the Culpeper Minute Battalion, on October 20th, caused something of a sensation. With tomahawks and scalping knives hanging from their belts, and "Liberty or Death" emblazoned on their fringed hunting shirts, the Minutemen presented a fearsome sight.[8] In fact, sixteen year old Philip Slaughter, a soldier in the Minute Battalion, recorded in his journal that,

> *"The people,* (of Williamsburg) *hearing that we were from the backwoods, and seeing our savage-looking equipment, seemed as much afraid of us as if we had been Indians."* [9]

Captain John Chilton

This was not the image that Captain John Chilton wished to present. As captain of a company of minutemen from Fauquier County, he wanted to demonstrate that neither he, nor his men, were the ill disciplined backwoodsmen that so many people assumed upon their arrival. To correct this false impression, and enhance his men's appearance, he went shopping about town. His purchases included 85 yards of oznaburg for hunting shirts, 44 yards of blue ½ thicks for leggins, a pound of thread, and dozens of small and large horn buttons. He also took care of his own uniform needs, obtaining the necessary

---

[8] Rev. Philip Slaughter, A History of St. Mark's Parish : Culpeper County Virginia (1877), 107
[9] Ibid.

4

material for a fine regimental coat.[10]   At age 36, respectability
was clearly important to Captain Chilton.

He had long ago earned the respect of his neighbors in
Fauquier County.   He served in such important positions as
church vestryman, justice of the peace, and lieutenant in the
county militia.   Although he was a land surveyor by trade,
most of his attention was devoted to the management of his
590 acre estate with its numerous slaves.[11]   His standing in the
community had also been enhanced in 1768 by his marriage to
seventeen year old Lettice Blackwell, a member of a
prominent family in the county.   The marriage had actually
been planned two years earlier when Lettice was only fifteen
and John twenty-five.[12]   Apparently it was a happy one,
producing five children in seven years.[13]

In the fall of 1775, however, Captain Chilton's attention
centered on his company of minute-men.   They had marched
to Williamsburg to help counter the threat from Lord Dunmore
and when they arrived they were both anxious and excited
about the impending conflict.   These sentiments soon gave
way to restlessness however, as weeks passed without any
significant confrontation.   The Minutemen chafed at their
inactivity and resented the military discipline of camp life.
Militia musters of the past had typically been short affairs,
after which the men returned to their comfortable homes.
Camp life in Williamsburg, however, was anything but
comfortable.   The monotony was occasionally broken by

[10] Mary Goodwin, Clothing and Accoutrements of the Officers and
Soldiers of the Virginia Forces : 1775-1780 (Unpublished, 1962), 44
(Half Thicks were a coarse wool material. Leggins were leg wraps
meant to protect one's socks and legs)
[11] A September 1778 inventory of Chilton's estate lists ten slaves,
valued from 200 to 30 pounds and totally 1,140 pounds. See Dee
Ann Buck's Abstracts of Fauquier County Virginia: Wills, Inventories
and Accounts 1759-1799 (1998), 11
[12] T. Tripplett Russell and John K. Gott, Fauquier County in the
Revolution (Westminster, MD : Willow Bend Books, 1988), 89
[13] Ibid. 100

skirmishes at Hampton and Kemp's Landing, but these were relatively minor incidents.

Battle of Great Bridge

The big showdown between Lord Dunmore and the Virginians occurred in December, at a place called Great Bridge. The village was located twelve miles south of Norfolk and was named for the long wooden bridge and causeway that crossed the southern branch of the Elizabeth River. Upon learning that Lord Dunmore had established a base of operations at Norfolk, the Virginia Convention sent a force to confront him. Captain Chilton and his men, along with four other companies of the Culpeper Minute Battalion and six companies of the 2nd Virginia Regiment, totaling 800 men in all, marched to Great Bridge in early December.[14]

When they arrived, they found that Dunmore had built a small fort near the northern end of the bridge. It covered the road to Norfolk, and was derisively named the "Hog Pen" by the Virginians. Captain Chilton and the rest of the Virginians erected breastworks on the opposite side of the bridge and causeway. Lord Dunmore had just 250 men to defend the fort, including approximately 100 regulars from the 14th Regiment and some British Marines.[15] They also had a couple of small cannon that could sweep the bridge with grapeshot. The Virginians, lacking cannon of their own, were unable to inflict much damage on the fort and declined to mount a frontal assault. As a result, the two sides just sniped at each other for over a week.

The stalemate finally ended on the morning of December 9th with a sudden attack by the British. Lord Dunmore, fearing reports that reinforcements with cannon were about to join the Virginians, decided to strike before they arrived. The

---

[14] Ibid.
[15] Ibid. 83

attack began with an early morning fusillade of British gunfire that Captain Chilton and the rest of the Virginians largely ignored.

> *"As the enemy had paid us this compliment several times before"*, one Virginian officer wrote, *"we at first concluded (*the firing*) to be nothing more than a morning salute."*[16]

Soon, however, the Virginians were startled to see a column of redcoats, with bayonets fixed, marching six abreast across the bridge. Future Supreme Court Chief Justice John Marshall, a nineteen year old lieutenant in the Culpeper Minute Battalion, wrote that,

> *"The alarm was immediately given and, as is the practice of raw troops, the bravest rushed to the works where, regardless of order, they kept up a heavy fire on the front of the British column."*[17]

Many of the men in the works were Culpeper Minutemen under the command of Marshall's father, Major Thomas Marshall. Another group of Minutemen, armed with rifles, were positioned on high ground to the left of the causeway. From this spot the riflemen were able to fire into the right flank of the British.[18] The Virginians put forth a devastating fire that quickly shattered the enemy's advance. Captain Charles Fordyce, commanding the British assault, fell with 14

---

[16] Letter of Major Spottswood, in <u>John Marshall : Definer of a Nation</u>, by Jean Edward Smith, (New York : Holt Inc.,, 1996), 49
[17] John Marshall, <u>The Life of George Washington : Vol. 2</u>, (Fredericksburg, VA: The Citizen's Guild of Washington's Boyhood Home, 1926), 132
[18] Jean Edward Smith, <u>John Marshall : Definer of a Nation</u>, (New York : Holt Inc., 1996), 49

bullets in him.[19] The rest of his force faired little better. They withdrew to the fort thoroughly bloodied. Lieutenant John Marshall proudly wrote that,

> *"Every grenadier is said to have been killed or wounded in this ill-judged attack, while the Americans did not lose a single man."*[20]

That night Lord Dunmore evacuated the fort and soon after, Norfolk, once again seeking the safety of British ships. Although he still remained a threat, the Virginians were very pleased. Colonel William Woodford, the overall commander of Virginia's forces at Great Bridge, boasted that the battle, *"was a second Bunker's Hill affair, in miniature, with this difference, that we kept our post."*[21]

Captain Chilton and his men undoubtedly felt the same elation. They had withstood their first test of battle nicely. Chilton's joy, however, was short lived, for soon after the battle he received tragic news that his wife had died. He immediately rushed home to tend to his family.

The next few months were filled with great sadness for Captain Chilton and his children. By all accounts, he had cared deeply for his wife; more than a year after her death, he still wrote fondly of her in letters from the battlefields of the north. Little is known, however, about how he dealt with his loss that winter, and by April of 1776, he was back in military service. His brother Charles and sister-in-law Betsy, who lived on an adjoining estate, agreed to take care of his five children, his slaves, and his land.[22]

[19] Ibid.
[20] Marshall, 132
[21] Selby, 74
[22] Russell and Gott, 100

The 3rd Virginia Regiment

Over the winter, while Captain Chilton was occupied with family matters, the Virginia Convention increased the number of regular, (full time) regiments, from two to eight. The 3rd Virginia Regiment, commanded by Hugh Mercer of Fredericksburg, was one of these new units. It was raised in Fauquier and the surrounding counties of northern Virginia.[23] During the spring of 1776, while he mourned the loss of his wife, John Chilton also recruited the necessary quota of men to warrant a Captain's commission in the 3rd Virginia. His commission was dated April 29, 1776.[24]

It is unclear precisely when Chilton's company joined the regiment. Since the 3rd Virginia spent most of the spring in Alexandria and Dumfries, it is likely that, by early May, Chilton's company arrived at one of these locations. At the time, the regiment was stationed along the Potomac River, keeping a lookout for Lord Dunmore. George Mason, of Fairfax County, was relieved to have such a force in the area, writing to General Washington in early April that,

> *"A regiment commanded by Colonel Mercer of Fredericksburg, is stationed on this part of the river, and I hope we shall be tolerably safe, unless a push is made here with a large body of men."*[25]

Colonel Mercer, however, was not as upbeat about the situation. In a April 14th letter to General Charles Lee -- the

---

[23] E. M. Sanchez-Saavedra, <u>A Guide to Virginia Military Organizations in the American Revolution : 1774 – 1787</u> (Richmond : Virginia State Library, 1978), 39
[24] Ibid.
[25] George Mason to General George Washington, 2 April, 1776 in Kate Mason Rowland's <u>The Life and Correspondence of George Mason Vol. 1</u> (New York: Russell & Russell, 1964), 219

recently arrived commander of southern forces -- Mercer reported that the town of Alexandria,

> "...*appears to me to be the principal object we are to attend to in defence of the frontier along the Potowmack River. Guards will also be necessary on Ocquaquan, Quantico, & Patowmack Creeks. I should judge that my Regiment cannot occupy further along that Frontier without dividing us too much...Three Companies of my Regiment are on duty at Hampton...We remain very ill provided with arms: the two Companies from Fauquier have not yet joined the Regiment.*"[26]

Fortunately for Colonel Mercer and his men, the duty was uneventful, and by early June, the 3rd Virginia was ordered to Williamsburg.

They were needed there, because in late May, Lord Dunmore landed troops on Gwynn's Island. The island was located just off the mainland, near the mouth of the Rappahannock River in the Chesapeake Bay. Dunmore believed it was a good site from which to resume his operations. Within a day of his landing, however, troops from the 7th Virginia Regiment arrived and took up positions directly across from the island.[27] A narrow strip of water was all that separated the two forces. A stalemate ensued for most of June as both sides dug in. By early July, the Virginians, commanded by General Andrew Lewis, were ready to attack. They brought up a number of cannon and commenced a bombardment on July 9th.

[26] Colonel Hugh Mercer to General Charles Lee, 14 April, 1776, in The Lee Papers, vol.1 (Collections of the New York Historical Society, 1871), 419

[27] Brigadier General Andrew Lewis to General Charles Lee, 3 June, 1776, in The Lee Papers, vol.2 (Collections of the New York Historical Society, 1871), 52

Already ravaged by an outbreak of smallpox, the unexpectedly heavy cannon barrage broke the will of the besieged Governor. He evacuated the island that evening, leaving behind many disease ridden corpses, as well as a number of escaped slaves who had been promised their freedom if they joined him. They were sick with smallpox and could serve no useful purpose to the Governor.

It is likely that a portion of the 3rd Virginia, possibly even Chilton's company, participated in the action at Gwynn's Island. In a letter dated June 12th to General Charles Lee (who had left Virginia a month earlier for Charleston South Carolina), General Lewis reported that, *"I have sent under the Command of Col. Mercer three companies to reinforce Col. Dangerfield's Battalion."*[28]

If members of the 3rd Virginia were at Gwynn's Island though, they did not stay long, for the regiment spent the latter half of July in Williamsburg. At the end of the month the 3rd Virginia was sent back to the Potomac to once again keep watch for Dunmore. This time they were stationed in Westmoreland County, about fifty miles down river from Dumfries. Once again they found the duty tedious and uneventful. On August 4th, the regiment's new commander, Colonel George Weedon, who replaced newly promoted General Hugh Mercer, complained that,

"The extreme heat, Dirty roads, cursed ferrys, d—n musketeers, and one plague or other has almost cracked my brain...Our business here was to Counteract Dunmore in his Motions."[29]

[28] Brigadier General Andrew Lewis to General Charles Lee, 12 June, 1776 in <u>The Lee Papers</u>, vol. 2 (Collections of the New York Historical Society, 1871), 63

[29] Weedon letter to John Page, 4 August, 1776 in Harry M. Ward, <u>Duty, Honor, or Country : General George Weedon and the American Revolution</u> (Philadelphia : American Philosophical Society, 1979), 55

Unbeknownst to Weedon though, Dunmore's fleet had sailed out of the Chesapeake a few days earlier. Half of the fleet headed for Florida to reinforce a garrison there. Lord Dunmore sailed with the remaining ships to New York, just in time to meet General William Howe's invasion force on Staten Island. The 3rd Virginia spent one more week along the Potomac River before they too headed north to join General Washington's army in New York.[30]

The stage was set for a major confrontation. The only question was, would the 3rd Virginia arrive in time to participate?

---

[30] Ward, 56

Eastern Virginia

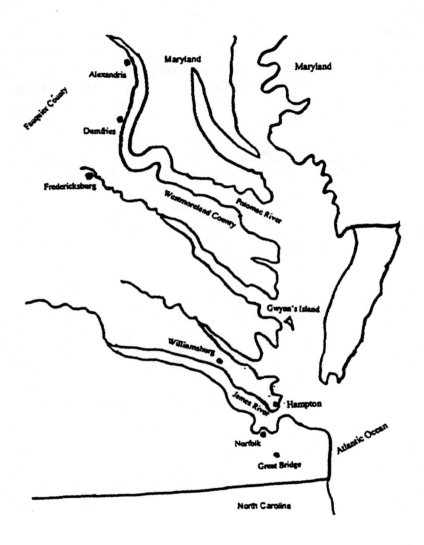

Chapter Two

"Tell the Fathers of My Brave Boys Their Sons Are Soldiers"

The 3rd Virginia Arrives in New York

The 3rd Virginia's long march north covered over 400 miles in 26 days.[1] Along the way, news reached them of the American defeat at Long Island. Shocking as this was, the Americans were fortunate that General Howe, the British commander, declined to press his attack. As a result, the bulk of Washington's army escaped across the East River to Manhattan Island. Over the next few weeks both sides remained largely stationary as each prepared for General Howe's next move.

When Chilton's regiment finally joined Washington's army, on September 13th, it was greeted with tremendous excitement, for much was expected of the Virginians.[2] As soon as they settled in camp, Captain Chilton wrote a quick letter to his father-in-law, Joseph Blackwell.

---

[1] Russell and Gott, 112

[2] John Chilton to Joseph Blackwell, 13 September, 1776, In Lyon Tyler's, " The Old Virginia Line in the Middle States During the American Revolution", <u>Tyler's Quarterly Historical and Genealogical Magazine vol. 12</u>, (Richmond, VA: Richmond Press Inc., 1931), 91 The letters and diary of Captain John Chilton are included in the article.

> "...*our Regiment have reached this place in good
> spirits and generally speaking healthy, tho not quite
> full, however; great joy was expressed at our arrival
> and great things expected from the Virginians, and of
> consequence we must go through great fatigue and
> danger.*"[3]

Chilton noted that they were camped on the northern end of
Manhattan Island, near Kings Bridge, about fourteen miles
above the town of New York. He worried that since they were
on an island, with a massive British fleet offshore, and a large
army poised to strike at any moment, they might soon find
themselves trapped. He could see the British encampments on
Long Island and the flash from their cannon as they fired
across the East River. The British maintained a steady
bombardment all day, prompting Chilton to complain that he
had to write hurriedly.[4]

In the evening a British party was discovered landing on a
small island in the East River. As a result, much of the
American army, including the 3rd Virginia, manned their alarm
posts all night. Captain Chilton and his men marched and
counter-marched into the early morning hours of September
14th, returning to camp at sunrise. The remainder of the day
was relatively quiet, but at midnight they were once again
called out to their alarm posts to repeat the actions of the night
before.[5]

Returning to camp on the morning of the 15th, the
thoroughly exhausted Virginians indulged themselves with
breakfast. As they finished their meal, word arrived that the
enemy had landed at Kip's Bay, a few miles below their
location. It was reported throughout the camp that the

---

[3] Ibid
[4] Ibid.
[5] John Chilton to friends, 17 September, 1776 in <u>Tyler's Quarterly</u>,
92

American forces posted at Kip's Bay had shamefully abandoned their position without firing a shot.[6] As a result, the town of New York easily fell to the enemy.

The 3rd Virginia once more manned its alarm post in anticipation of an enemy assault. Captain Gustuvus Wallace, commanding a company of 3rd Virginians from King George County, wrote home a few days later saying that,

> *"though our regiment had been out of camp under arms for two nights before, we were ordered to cover the retreat of the cowardly Yankeymen... "[7]*

His fellow captain, John Chilton, reported that the men were ready for battle.

> *"Our soldiers were greatly exasperated and being drawn up for Battle, it was very discoverable that they were determined to fight to the last for their country; every soldier encouraging and animating his fellow"[8]*

Battle of Harlem Heights

Although the British attack at Kip's Bay caught the Americans by surprise and met little resistance, the enemy once again failed to press their advantage. As a result, most of the American forces stationed on the southern half of Manhattan were able to retire northward, to the fortifications of Harlem Heights, before the British severed the roads. Captain Chilton's company, along with the rest of the 3rd

---

[6] Ibid.
[7] Gustuvus Wallace to his brother, 17 September, 1777 in <u>Tyler's Quarterly</u>, 94
[8] John Chilton to friends, 17 September, 1777 in Tyler's Quarterly, 92

Virginia, manned these fortifications and watched American soldiers straggle in all night. By midnight the British established their own line of fortifications, opposite the ones at Harlem Heights.

Early the next morning, British troops fired upon a detachment of New England rangers who had moved into no-man's land between the two lines.[9] The rangers, commanded by Colonel Thomas Knowlton of Connecticut, held their ground for thirty minutes before retiring in the face of overpowering numbers.[10] The firing attracted General Washington's attention and he soon arrived to take personal command. Observing an opportunity to exploit the enemy's aggressiveness, he issued orders that placed the Americans on the offensive.

A detachment was ordered forward to engage and hold the enemy, while a second detachment worked its way around the flank, using the woods as cover, to strike the enemy in the rear. If all went as planned, the British advance troops would be cut off from their main line and trapped between two American units.

The 3rd Virginia played an important role in both detachments. Its three rifle companies were attached to the flanking force while the remaining line companies – seven in all, including Captain Chilton's – joined the holding force. Chilton described what happened in a letter the next day.

"(In the) *morning we marched down toward* (the enemy) *and posted ourselves near a meadow having that to our front,* (the) *No. river to our right, a body of woods in our rear and on our left. We discovered the enemy peeping from their Heights over their*

---

[9] Philip Katcher, "They Behaved Like Soldiers: The Third Virginia Regiment at Harlem Heights", <u>Virginia Cavalcade</u>, (Vol. 26, No. 2, Autumn 1976), 64

[10] Ibid.

fencings and rocks and running backwards and forwards. We did not alter our positions. I believe they expected we should have ascended the hill to them, but finding us still, they imputed it to fear and came down skipping towards us in small parties. At a distance of 250 or 300 yards they began their fire. Our orders were not to fire till they came near but a young officer (of whom we have too many) on the right fired and it was taken up from right to left. We made about 4 fires ... We then all wiped and loaded and sat down in our ranks and let the enemy fire on us near an hour. "[11]

While British attention focused on the Americans in their front, the three Virginia rifle companies, commanded by Major Andrew Leitch – along with Connecticut rangers under Colonel Knowlton -- moved around the enemy to hit them in the rear. Unfortunately, when this force initiated their attack, they were not behind, but rather on the right flank of the British. Despite this miscue, the riflemen and rangers -- joined by the detachment in front of the enemy -- fought with such tenacity that the British were compelled to retreat. They reformed on top of a hill further back. General George Clinton of New York commented that,

"...We (the attacking Americans) pursued them to a buckwheat field on top of a high hill, the distance about four hundred paces, where they received a considerable re-enforcement, with several field-pieces, and there made a stand. A very brisk action ensued at this place which continued about two

---

[11] John Chilton to friends, 17 September, 1776, in <u>Tyler's Quarterly</u>, 93

18

hours.   Our people at length worsted them a third time."[12]

David Griffith, the regimental surgeon for the 3rd Virginia, proudly described the role of the 3rd Virginia in a letter home.

"A very smart action ensued in the true Bush-fighting way....our Troops behaved in a manner that does them the highest Honor. After keeping a very heavy fire on both sides for near three hours they drove the enemy to their main Body and then were prudently ordered to retreat for fear of being drawn into an ambuscade.   The 3rd Virga. Regt. (Weedon's) was ordered out at the Beginning to maintain a particular post in front, and Major Leitch was detached with the 3 Rifle Companies to flank the Enemy. He conducted himself on this occasion in a manner that does him the greatest honor and so did his Party, till he received two balls in his Belly and one In his hip...We had 3 men killed and ten wounded. The Loudon (County) Company suffered most − the Captain behaved nobly. Our whole loss is not yet ascertained. The wounded are not more than 40. Coll. Noleton (Knowlton) of the N.E. Rangers is the only officer killed. ...Our Battalion (after the Riflemen were detached) were attacked in open field which they drove off and forced them down a Hill...I must mention that the two Yankee Regts. who ran on Sunday fought tollerably well on Monday and in some measure retrieved their reputation. This affair, tho' not great in itself, is of consequence as it gives spirits to the army, which they wanted. Indeed the

---

[12] Henry P. Johnston, <u>The Battle Of Harlem Heights</u>, (London : Macmillian, 1897), 80

confusion was such on Sunday that everybody looked dispirited. At present everything wears a different face. "[13]

Captain Chilton was also proud of his men, writing to his brother that,

"Our men observed the best order, not quitting their ranks tho exposed to a constant warm fire. I can't say enough in their favour, they behaved like soldiers who fought from principle alone... Tell the old Planters in Fauqr their sons are fine fellows and soldiers."[14]

Even General Washington expressed satisfaction with the conduct of the troops, thanking them in the next day's general orders.[15] After defeats at Long Island and Kips Bay, the victorious skirmish at Harlem Heights helped bolster American morale. And although American spirits were dampened with the loss of both Colonel Knowlton and Major Leitch, as well as approximately 100 men killed and wounded, the fact that they inflicted an equal number of casualties and took the field from the British had a very positive effect on the troops.[16]

---

[13] David Griffith to Major Leven Powell, 18 September, 1776 in Johnston's, The Battle of Harlem Heights, 171-172
The Mr. Griffith cited by Johnston is incorrectly identified as being a Colonel from Maryland when in fact David Griffith of the 3rd Virginia carried on a frequent correspondence with Major Leven Powell during the war.
[14] John Chilton to friends, 17 September, 1776, in Tyler's Quarterly, 93
[15] General Orders of the Continental Army, 16 September, 1777 (The George Washington Papers at the Library of Congress : Online)
[16] Johnston, 87

New York

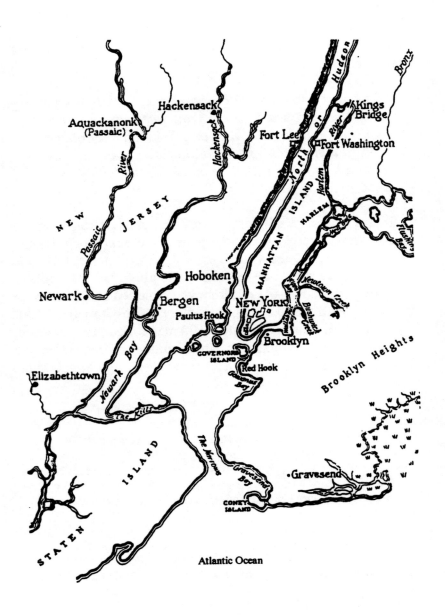

White Plains to the Delaware

Over the next few weeks the situation remained relatively quiet, as neither side wished to attack the strong fortifications of the other. Nevertheless, there were indications in the British camp that something was brewing. Captain Chilton, writing on October 4th, observed that,

> "...*the Enemy have been peaceable but seem vastly busy and we expect something every hour. We are on our guard and our men seem resolutely bent to give them a warm reception at the meeting. The Yankees, who were timorous when we first came here, have plucked up a heart and I hope will fight lustily.*"[17]

Chilton noted that although the men had plenty of good beef, there was little else of variety to eat.

> "*Our men have been sickly with Fevers and agues but are now mending...and tho we are between two rivers we get no fish and very few oysters or clams or cockles...We sometimes get Pork and Pease, Rum, Brandy &c.*"[18]

Two days later he added,

> "*We have just removed from our old encampment about ½ mile into the wood where we are building like Moonacks in the ground, nothing has yet happened. We send out scouting parties for the plank we want for our hovels, cabbages, apples, &c.*"[19]

---

[17] John Chilton to friends, 4 October, 1776, in <u>Tyler's Quarterly</u>, 96
[18] Ibid.
[19] Ibid.

Chilton also observed that as the American army grew more daring, the enemy seemed to become more cautious.

"I begin to think that mankind when engaged in warfare are as wary and timorous of each other as deer are of men, and the boldness of one party increases as they find the other fearful. After the battle we were very cautious of encroaching too far on the Enemy's sentinels, but we have, as it were by stealth, pushed them from one post to another until they have hardly ground to stand on without their fortifications. An attachment of 100 men under Genl. Putnam (of Virginians) went last night and foraged in the teeth of the Enemy who chose to let them take all they wanted without being so ill natured as to give one fire."[20]

Chilton believed though, that British caution would only last so long.

"There came over a deserter to us this morning from the Enemy and our scouts made two prisoners. We must fight soon, the Ministerials pride will be roused at many of these impertinences."[21]

Chilton's prediction proved all too true as General Howe resumed the offensive in mid October. He attempted to trap Washington's army on Manhattan Island by landing on the mainland at Pell's Point and marching to King's Bridge, the only bridge off of Manhattan Island. Fortunately for the Americans, Colonel John Glover, of Massachusetts, commanded a small force that delayed the British long enough

---

[20] Ibid.
[21] Ibid.

to allow General Washington to reposition the bulk of his army on the mainland, near White Plains.

On October 22nd, troops from the 3rd Virginia participated in a sharp skirmish with Tory Rangers a few miles from White Plains. A week later, on October 28th, the main armies clashed. Since most of the fighting occurred on Chatterton's Hill, a good distance from their position, the Virginians were largely spectators to the battle. Those Americans who did fight inflicted a number of casualties on the enemy. Nevertheless, the British took the hill, forcing General Washington to withdraw northward[22]

The strain of the campaign was starting to show on the Americans. The commander of the 3rd Virginia, Colonel Weedon, reported in a letter in late October that,

> *"the suffering of my poor men makes me feel exceedingly, for these five weeks we have been under arms every morning before day, exclusive of the other necessary duties of the army, which has been uncommonly hard, they have obliged to engage it, entirely naked, some without shoes or stockings several without blankets and almost all without shirts."*[23]

A November 5th troop return for the 3rd Virginia reported only 290 men out of 603 present and fit for duty.[24] This was typical for the entire American army. Fortunately they received an unexpected respite when General Howe suddenly broke off contact and returned to Manhattan Island.

---

[22] Craig L. Symonds, A Battlefield ATLAS of the American Revolution (The Nautical & Aviation Publishing Co. of America Inc., 1986), 29

[23] George Weedon to Page, 26 October, 1776 in Ward's, Duty, Honor, or Country, 66

[24] Return of the Third Virginia Regiment, 5 November, 1776, in Peter Force's, American Archive : 5th Series, (1837), 515-516

In an attempt to prevent the British from using the Hudson River, General Washington had left a large garrison at Fort Washington, on the northern end of Manhattan Island. After the battle at White Plains, General Howe decided to deal with this threat in his rear, marching his army back to Manhattan and attacking the fort. There was little General Washington could do to assist the garrison and it fell on November 15th with over 2800 prisoners. General Howe then returned his attention to Washington, who had divided his army. Six thousand American soldiers remained in New York under General Charles Lee while the rest, barely 3,500 men crossed the Hudson River with Washington.[25] On November 18th, the British followed, crossing the Hudson, capturing Fort Lee, and resuming their pursuit of Washington's tiny army.

As November came to a close General Washington's situation continued to deteriorate. With the British close on their heels the American army steadily retreated across New Jersey. On November 27th Chilton's regiment, serving in the rear guard, passed through Elizabethtown. He described the march in a letter.

> *"(On the) 27th, all the forces came through Elizabeth on their way to Brunswick. Our Regmt. brought up the rear. This was a melancholy day, deep miry road and so many men to tread it made it very disagreeable marching, we came 8 or 10 miles and encamped. Yesterday, we reached this place. How long we shall stay, I can't say, but expect we shall make a stand near this place if not at it, but no certainty when the Enemy are advancing on and an engagement may happen before tomorrow night. We*

---

[25] Symonds, 29

must fight to a disadvantage. They exceed us in numbers greatly."[26]

The once formidable American army had dwindled to only a few thousand stalwarts. Chilton wrote to his brother that he couldn't explain what happened to the, *"good army of Americans you were told we had."*[27] Perhaps they had been but an illusion. He decried the short enlistments of the militia as one source of the problem.

> *" O, god that our Congress should raise men just for an expense till time comes for them to fight and then their time be out!"*[28]

Yet, despite the hardship, Chilton remained surprisingly optimistic. He continued to his brother,

> *"You may guess we are in some confusion, and yet let me tell you not so much as you may imagine...Genl. Lee is yet in N. York with 10 or 12000 but fear he can't join us in time, and indeed, I don't know whether he should come to our assistance. If he should and we get them a little further in the Country we could shortly give a good account of ourselves and them too, I trust, but if the Militia joins us in a day or two, I hope they will repent their bold step. Our men are very willing to fight them on any terms but our generals are the best judges when it is best to be done."*[29]

---

[26] John Chilton to his brother, 30 November, 1776, in <u>Tyler's Quarterly</u>, 98

[27] Ibid.

[28] Ibid.

[29] Ibid.

Chilton wasn't as supportive, however, of recent promotions in the army. Apparently, men who were still in Virginia were being promoted ahead of him and his junior officers. He bitterly wrote that,

> *"If men were to be particularly preferred for seeing service where was Isham Keith, John Blackwell and Joe,* (officers in his regiment) *who have seen more service in one month than he, the Capt. could see in Williamsburg in an age."*[30].

It is unclear who Chilton was referring to back in Williamsburg, but clearly he took issue with the way promotions were decided. It particularly angered him that the difficult service that he and his men performed on campaign did not seem to count any more than service in Virginia, although it had been months since Virginia had even been threatened, much less attacked.

He closed his letter with kind words for his sister-in-law, Betsy. She had cared for his five children and supervised his servants since the spring and Captain Chilton was concerned about the burden this placed on her. He asked,

> *"How shall I thank Betsy for the great pains she takes with my dear little ones in clothing them and my Negroes, she has more than she can do. It will kill her, so pray my brother, get a good girl or Negro wench and I will pay for hire and take anything from my plantation that you stand in need of. There are two good smart steers, get corn from my house and make Gafney* (the overseer) *fatten one or both for you. Use everything as your own."*[31]

---

[30] Ibid. 99
[31] Ibid.

By early December the American army was in desperate straits. They simply could not stand against the pursuing British and were chased completely across New Jersey. On December 7th Washington's troops crossed the Delaware River into Pennsylvania. Charles Wilson Peale, a lieutenant in the Pennsylvania Militia, described the scene.

"All the shores were lighted up with large fires, boats continually passing and repassing, full of men, horses, artillery and camp equipage. The sick and half naked veterans of the long retreat streamed past. I thought it the most hellish scene I ever beheld...Suddenly a man staggered out of the line and came towards me. He had lost all of his clothes. He was in an old dirty blanket-jacket, his beard was long and his face full of sores...which so disfigured him that he was not known by me on first sight. Only when he spoke did I recognize my brother James."[32]

Fortunately for the Americans, General Washington had the foresight to collect every boat within seventy miles of Trenton. When the British arrived at the river, they had no way to cross. For the time being the remnants of Washington's army were safe. Scattered along the western shore of the river, the men struggled to stay warm and find food. Lieutenant Enoch Anderson of the Delaware Regiment, described his first night in Pennsylvania.

"...we lay amongst the leaves without tents or blankets, laying down with our feet to the fire. We had nothing to cook with but our ramrods, which we

[32] William Dwyer, The Day Is Ours! : An Inside View of the Battles of Trenton and Princeton, November 1776 – January 1777, (New Brunswick, New Jersey : Rutgers University Press, 1983), 102, 105

run through a piece of meat and roasted it over the fire, and to hungry soldiers it tasted sweet."[33]

Captain Chilton and the 3rd Virginia were posted in the same area, a few miles above McKonkey's Ferry. They undoubtedly experienced similar conditions. David Griffith, the regimental surgeon, described the situation on December 8th, writing that,

"…we have much need for a speedy re-inforcement. I am much afraid we shall not have it in time to prevent the destruction of American affairs… Everything here wears the face of despondency…A strange consternation seems to have seized everybody in this country. A universal dissatisfaction prevails, and everybody is furnished with an excuse for declining the publick service."[34]

Thomas Paine summed up the situation best with his memorable words, *"These are the times that Try Men's Souls."* The summer soldier and sunshine patriots had indeed abandoned the cause, and all that was left were a few thousand hearty souls, clinging to the west bank of the Delaware River. Even General Washington was concerned, writing to his brother on December 18th that,

[33] Richard Ketchum, The Winter Soldiers : The Battles for Trenton and Princeton, (New York : Henry Holt & Co., 1973), 115
[34] David Griffith to Major Powell, 8 December, 1776 in Tyler's Quarterly, 101

"...our Affairs are in a very bad situation...In a word my dear Sir, if every nerve is not strain'd to recruit the New Army with all possible expedition, I think the game is pretty near up..."[35]

For almost three weeks Captain Chilton and his cold and hungry men, braced themselves for an anticipated British crossing. Rumors spread around camp that the enemy was waiting for the river to freeze and then planned to walk across at their leisure. Many wondered if there would even be an American army left to challenge them. An American force return for December 22nd showed the 3rd Virginia with less than 200 men fit for duty.[36] The total effective force that General Washington had at his disposal was only around 6,500 men.[37] Many of these, however, were militia forces posted miles away. Only about 2,400 men were available for General Washington's immediate use. With the enlistments for most of the army due to expire at the end of the year, General Washington knew that a bold stroke was necessary to bolster morale, and maybe even save the cause.

---

[35] Gen. Washington to John A. Washington, 18, December, 1776 (The George Washington Papers at the Library of Congress : Online)
[36] Return of the Forces in the Service of the United States of American Encamped and in Quarters on the Banks of the Delaware, 22 December, 1776, American Archives (5th Series, vol. III), 1401-02
[37] Russell and Gott 136

Chapter Three

"Our Troops...Have Given Great Annoyance to the Enemy"

Battle of Trenton

General Washington's bold stroke came on December 26th. Hoping to catch the 1,400 man Hessian garrison at Trenton by surprise, General Washington devised a daring, multi-pronged attack. He would lead the remains of the continental army, just 2,400 men, across the Delaware River, nine miles above Trenton. Two smaller detachments of Pennsylvania militia were to cross the river below Trenton. They would all then converge on the town, entrapping the Hessians and giving the Americans a much-needed victory. The key to the operation was surprise. Washington hoped that an attack on the day after Christmas would catch the Hessians off guard. It was also important to coordinate the attack so that all the American units hit Trenton just before sunrise. This meant that the river crossing had to occur at night.

On Christmas Day orders were given to cook three days provisions, draw new flints and ammunition, and prepare to march.[1] The crossing commenced just after sunset. An officer on Washington's staff, probably Colonel John Fitzgerald, formerly of the 3rd Virginia, gave a detailed description of the crossing in his diary.

---

[1] General Mercer to Col. Durkee, 25 December, 1776 in William Stryker's. The Battles of Trenton and Princeton, (Republished by The Old Barracks Assoc., Trenton NJ : 2001, Originally published in 1898), 362

"Christmas, 6 p.m. -- ...It is fearfully cold and raw and a snow-storm setting in. The wind is northeast and beats in the faces of the men. It will be a terrible night for the soldiers who have no shoes. Some of them have tied old rags around their feet; others are barefoot, but I have not heard a man complain. They are ready to suffer any hardship and die rather than give up their liberty."[2]

Nine hours later, from across the river, the same officer wrote,

"Dec. 26, 3 a.m. -- I am writing in the ferry house. The troops are all over, and the boats have gone back for the artillery. We are now three hours behind the set time. Glover's men (from Massachusetts) *have had a hard time to force the boats through the floating ice with the snow drifting in their faces. I never have seen Washington so determined as he is now. He stands on the bank of the river, wrapped in his cloak, superintending the landing of the troops. He is calm and collected, but very determined. The storm is changing to sleet, and cuts like a knife. The last cannon is being landed, and we are ready to mount our horses."*[3]

Washington's force started its march on Trenton around 4:00 a.m., four hours behind schedule.[4] Although Washington did not know it at the time, the American units below Trenton had an even harder time crossing the river. They finally gave

---

[2] Diary of an American Officer on Washington's Staff, in Stryker, 360
[3] Ibid.
[4] Stryker, 139

up, assuming that General Washington had probably failed as well.

Far from failing, General Washington was more determined than ever to see the attack through, and the password for the day, "Victory or Death", emphasized this. Many of the officers displayed the same determination, urging the men to avenge the disasters at Long Island, New York, and New Jersey.[5] The raging winter storm made the march very difficult on the men. Nevertheless, they pressed forward. Major James Wilkenson, an aide to General Washington, recorded in his memoirs that,

> *"their route was easily traced, as there was a little snow on the ground, which was tinged here and there with blood from the feet of the men who wore broken shoes."*[6] General Washington himself noted that, *"Many of our poor soldiers are quite barefoot and ill-clad."*[7]

About mid-way to Trenton the column split, with General Sullivan leading half the men down the River road and General Greene taking the other half along the Pennington road. The plan called on them to enter Trenton simultaneously from two directions. But as dawn broke, the Americans were still miles from town and the element of surprise was in jeopardy. Retreat however, had its own risks, as the Hessians would most assuredly learn of Washington's movements and attack the Americans before Washington could get his whole army back across the river. Reports that the storm was ruining the men's gunpowder only added to the crisis. Yet, General Washington never wavered in his determination to attack.

---

[5] Ibid. 140
[6] Ibid. 129
[7] Ibid.

When informed about the wet powder, he responded with a blunt message to General Sullivan,

> *"... tell the general to use the bayonet and penetrate into the town; for the town must be taken and I am resolved to take it."*[8]

Fortunately, the same storm that delayed the Americans caused the Hessians to let down their guard and cancel the usual patrols outside of town. The first contact between the two sides occurred just outside Trenton, around 8:00 a.m. An aide to General Washington recorded what happened in his diary.

> *"It was just 8 o' clock. Looking down the road I saw a Hessian running out from the house. He yelled in Dutch and swung his arms. Three or four others came out with their guns. Two of them fired at us, but the bullets whistled over our heads. Some of General Stephens men rushed forward and captured two."*[9]

The Americans quickly pushed the Hessian pickets into Trenton and took position of the high ground overlooking the town's main streets. The startled Hessians attempted to form in the streets but were harassed by American artillery firing grapeshot. Nevertheless, the Hessians were able to man two of their own cannon and were about to return fire when Captain William Washington and Lieutenant James Monroe, both of the 3rd Virginia, led their men in a charge that captured the pieces. Both officers were wounded in the exchange, Monroe quite seriously in the shoulder.[10]

---

[8] Ibid. 140
[9] Ibid. 363
[10] Ibid. 164

   The Hessians suffered far worse, however, and retreated to an apple orchard just outside of town. They desperately tried to form their lines, but the intense American fire took such a toll on the officers, and caused so much confusion among the ranks, that it was impossible to do so.[11]   Trapped by the Assunpink Creek to their rear, and the Americans on their front and flanks, they soon had little choice but surrender. The Hessians suffered over one hundred men killed or wounded, including their commander, Colonel Rall, who died of his wounds the next day.[12]   American losses were incredibly light. Aside from Captain Washington and Lieutenant Monroe, only two other privates were reported injured.[13]   The attack was a staggering success for the Americans, garnering over 900 Hessian prisoners along with much needed supplies.[14]   More importantly, however, the victory provided a huge boost to American morale.

---

[11] Ibid. 186
[12] Ibid. 195
[13] Ibid. 196
[14] Ibid. 386

Battle of Trenton

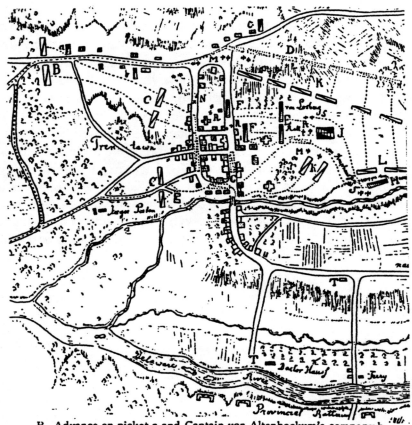

B. Advance on picket a and Captain von Altenbockum's company b.

C. Attack on Trenton after the retreat of the picket and Captain von Altenbockum's company, and also the captain's picket c, to Trenton.

D. March of the provincial troops in battalion formation.

E. March of the Hessian regiments after leaving Trenton.

F. Attack of the von Lossberg and Rall regiments on Trenton.

G. Provincial troops guarding the bridge.

H. Retreat of the von Knyphausen regiment at the time of the attack on the von Lossberg and Rall regiments.

J. Surrender of the von Lossberg and Rall regiments.

K. Attack on J by the provincial troops.

L. Attack on H after the surrender of the von Lossberg and Rall regiments.

M. Provincial artillery.

N. Rall cannon which were at once silenced.

R. Von Knyphausen cannon.

S. Von Lossberg cannon.

T. Commands which retreated to Burlington.

In order to preserve the victory, General Washington decided to withdraw across the Delaware River with the prisoners before the British could strike back. The weary American army marched back to McKonkey's Ferry, re-crossed the river and collapsed on the other side. It had been an exhausting, yet decisive two days.

As they slept, news of their victory spread throughout the region and beyond, restoring the flagging morale of Americans. Captain Chilton and the 3rd Virginia witnessed the renewed spirit of the populace first hand when they escorted the Hessian prisoners through the streets of Philadelphia on New Year's Day. As a result of this duty, it appears that Captain Chilton did not participate in the Battle of Princeton, a battle that cost the life of the 3rd Virginia's original commander, Hugh Mercer. This is not certain, however, because Chilton began a journal on January 3rd, the very day of the Princeton battle, and it implies that he, and presumably his company, were actually there. Unfortunately, he offers no specific details of his participation, and the general description he does provide is inaccurate in places.[15] Therefore, it is quite possible that he rejoined the army shortly after the battle at Princeton, and merely recorded what he was told about the events there.

Captain Chilton's journal reported that after the American victory at Princeton, the army *"marched with expedition towards the mountains,"* reaching Somerset Courthouse by evening. They resumed their march early the next morning, encamping at Pluckimin by nightfall. They dined on, *"plenty of Beef Pork,"* their first meal in nearly two days.[16] The army reached Morristown on January 6th where, according to Chilton, *"the 3rd Virga. Regt. were stationed 4 or 5 days on*

---

[15] Lyon Tyler, ed. <u>Tyler's Quarterly Historical and Genealogical Magazine,</u> vol. 12 no. 1, "The Old Virginia Line in the Middle States During the American Revolution: The Diary of Captain John Chilton, 3rd Virginia Regt.," July, 1930. 283

[16] Ibid.

(the) side of a Mountain without Tents. Ground covered with snow. "[17]

Morristown Encampment

As was the custom of the time, both armies suspended the campaign and settled into winter quarters. The 3rd Virginia stayed in the Morristown area until mid February when they marched to Hanover Township (Whippany) to be inoculated for small pox.

Captain Chilton reported that the regiment, *"had the small pox very lightly generally."* [18] They were not so fortunate with other illnesses however. Yellow and spotted fever, jaundice and several other ailments took their toll. Many of the men were allowed to leave camp to recuperate. Captain Chilton warned them to stay clear of Philadelphia, *"where death and every kind of disorder lay in ambush for them,"* yet that is where most ended up.[19]

Complicating matters for Chilton was the fact that command of the remnants of the 3rd Virginia, now well under 150 men, had devolved onto him. Colonel Weedon had been promoted to Brigadier General and assigned the task of Adjutant General, and the other staff officers and company captains were away from camp. Some were in Virginia recruiting, while others relaxed in nearby towns. Captain Chilton, writing to his brother on February 11th, lamented the condition and loss of his men. He was torn between tending to his sick in Philadelphia (and enjoying the comforts of the city) or staying in camp with the men who remained.

---

[17] Ibid.
[18] Ibid.
[19] John Chilton to his brother, 11 February, 1777 in <u>Tyler's Quarterly</u>, 112

*"The loss of my men gives me the greatest
uneasiness. If I could have been with them (in
Philadelphia) to have seen them well used, I could
bear it with great resignation, but I know they must
have suffered many wants, poor young fellows! I
sometimes blame myself for not going to them, for I
had leave. But what should I do. The poor lads who
had shared every danger with me begged I would not
leave them in the face of the enemy. The soldiers of
other companies also asked I should stay. My own
pride, and let me say reason, also told me it was not
the time to take pleasure so I left it to those who went
to take care of my sick. I hope they have done this
but I have not heard."* [20]

Captain Chilton even spent his own money to ease the
suffering of the men. He noted that,

*"The pay-master not making regular payments
distresses me too, for though I had enough money for
my own men, and to spare, (of those with me) yet I
find it very inconvenient for all, and yet, they look at
me for cash on every exigency. Indeed, some of their
Capts. have wrote to me to furnish their men with
money, and they, at the same time are out at some
town living in luxury or capering away to Virginia
while I, many times, scarcely know where my next
shirt is to be washed, and I can't see good soldiers
want."* [21]

Such genuine concern for the rank and file was certainly not
the norm in the strict social order of 18th century America.
Yet, time and again Chilton ignored class differences in favor

---

[20] Ibid. 113
[21] Ibid.

of his men's welfare. Their suffering weighed heavily on his mind.

Thankfully, by mid March, the causes of Captain Chilton's anxiety had decreased considerably. He wrote that aside from a small skirmish every few days, there was little to report. He described the British situation as somewhat desperate.

> *"The Conqueror of America finds himself, after all, his great conquest, in possession of a string of land inhabited by half-starved Tories, about 14 miles in length and one and a half in breadth, and but one way to make his escape and that is by way of Amboy...They now scarce dare creep out of their lines and when they do forage a little, our scouting parties precipitate them into their lines again, like hares before a hound. They have smallpox among them worse than we have...Their lines are so extensive that duty is excessive hard on them which gives them great colds and throws them into Pleurisies &c. They begin to desert over to us as fast as possible. "[22]*

The lull in activity caused Captain Chilton to turn his thoughts homeward. He wrote that,

> *"I greatly want to see Virginia and its inhabitants. No country yet like old Virginia! The women here from 16 years old have lost their teeth."[23]*

He then described the dress of Jersey women as not particularly to his liking. He concluded with, *"They don't live*

---

[22] John Chilton to Major Powell, 19, March, 1777, in <u>Tyler's Quarter</u>, 117
[23] Ibid

half as well as in Virginia, nor do they any where live so well."[24]

As winter subsided, and the weather and roads improved, General Washington grew concerned that the British were preparing to move against Philadelphia. As a result, he repositioned his scattered troops, including the 3rd Virginia, concentrating them near Middle Brook, a village that lay along a major road to Philadelphia.

General Washington also reorganized the army. On May 10th he wrote to Brigadier General William Woodford, giving him command of a newly formed brigade, made up of the 3rd, 7th, 11th, and 15th, Virginia regiments. Woodford had previously commanded the 2nd Virginia regiment from its inception in 1775 until September 1776, when he resigned in protest over being passed over for promotion. Although he had commanded the Virginia forces in their victory over Lord Dunmore at Great Bridge, Woodford alienated his men, and few re-enlisted after their one year of service expired. As a result, the 2nd Virginia was in disarray for a good part of 1776. In September of that year, with the 2nd regiment still floundering in Virginia, and other officers like Colonel Hugh Mercer, of the 3rd Virginia, being promoted ahead of him, Colonel Woodford resigned his commission. When Congress moved to enlarge the army in 1777, however, Colonel Woodford was offered the rank of Brigadier General. He

---

[24] Ibid.
[28] A General Return of the 12 Virginia Battalions in Morristown, May 17, 1777 (George Washington Papers at the Library of Congress: Online)

accepted this commission and was given command of the 3rd Virginia brigade.

In May 1777, Woodford's newly formed brigade was one in name only. The 15th Virginia regiment had not yet joined it and the total number of men from the other three did not amount to one complete regiment. On May 17th, the 3rd Virginia reported only 151 men fit for duty.[28] The other two regiments reported similar numbers. The 7th Virginia had 219 effectives while the 11th Virginia had only 185.[29] Sadly, these numbers were about average for all the continental regiments. Illness and fatigue had taken its toll on the army.

Despite such low numbers, some in the 3rd Virginia remained optimistic. David Griffith, reported on May 28th that the army had,

> *"given great annoyance to the Enemy* (all winter) *and prevented them from Plundering and Desolating the Country...the Troops begin to come in pretty fast, and I have been this day informed from good authority that by the 10th of June we shall have in this camp as least 12,000 effectives".*[30]

A troop return on May 21st, showed that Mr. Griffith's confidence was not misplaced. The total strength of the army was 8,188, nearly twice what it was in March.[31] The British however, had twice that number, and by June General Howe was finally ready to use them. On June 13th the British suddenly marched toward Princeton. The movement had every appearance of a major strike against the right wing of

---

[29] Ibid.

[30] David Griffith to Major Levin Powell, May 28, 1777 in Robert Powell's, <u>Biographical Sketch of Col. Levin Powell, 1737 – 1810: Including his Correspondence during the Revolutionary War,</u> (Alexandria, Virginia, G.H. Ramey & Son, 1877), 77

[31] Washington to Congress, 21 May, 1777 (George Washington Papers at the Library of Congress : Online)

the American army, to be followed by an advance on Philadelphia.

However, when the British advance suddenly halted, it became apparent to General Washington that General Howe's real design was to draw the Americans out of their lines and into a general engagement upon ground that was less advantageous to the Americans. Washington refused to take the bait, and on June 19th General Howe returned to his lines at Brunswick. He tried the same tactic a week later but once again General Washington refused to be fully drawn out of his fortified lines in the mountains. Some fighting did occur however. On June 26th, Colonel Daniel Morgan's Rifle Corps was almost surrounded by a sudden British advance. According to Captain Chilton, Morgan was able to lead his men out of the trap at the last minute, and when reinforcements under General Stirling arrived they,

> *"gave them (the British) so warm a reception that they were obliged to retreat so precipitately that it had like to have become a rout."*[32]

Captain Chilton soon found himself directly involved in the affair, marching to Bound Brook to confront a party of the enemy reported to be about 2,000 men strong.[33]

> *"We marched off with colors flying and drums beating which they hearing and expecting us were coming to attack them made their best of their way to Perth Amboy, since when they seem peaceably disposed and keep close."*[34]

---

[32] John Chilton to his brother, 29 June, 1777 in <u>Tyler's Quarterly</u>, 118
[33] Ibid.
[34] Ibid. 119

With the British back behind their earthworks, the Americans were given a brief respite. Captain Chilton found himself stationed in a mountain pass with thirty men and his very good friend, Captain William Blackwell. Captain Blackwell commanded a company of Fauquier County men in the 11th Virginia regiment. His Lieutenant was John Marshall, formerly of the Culpeper Minutemen.

Writing to his brother on June 29th, Captain Chilton reported that this guard duty station was, *"a pretty agreeable one…we are all hearty, few complaints being now in the Army of sickness."*[35] They were just two miles from the main encampment, so necessary items could be obtained from the camp. Yet, being away from camp made it easier for them to forage for such luxuries as milk and butter.

Near the end of his letter Captain Chilton turned his attention to his family.

> *"Tell the children I have some hopes of seeing them this fall, as there is some talk of our Regmt. being sent home in order to recruit and enlist the old soldiers again. Tis thought by this piece of indulgence they will enter the Service again (But keep this secret)."*[36]

He concluded with a request for Mr. Gafney, to take good care of his colt. With the inflated prices and low pay of the army, he didn't expect to return home with much money and he wanted to make sure that he at least had a good horse to ride.

On July 3rd, the 3rd Virginia marched to Morristown, where they stayed until July 12th. Captain Chilton, enjoying the relative calm of these ten days, wrote to a friend, Captain William Pickett in Fauquier County. He first gently

---

[35] Ibid. 118
[36] Ibid. 119

reprimanded him for not writing, and then complained about military promotions.

> *"Here I am 300 miles away from home, under the mortifying circumstances of being called 'Old Chilton' by the whole Army and seeing boys whom I would not have made Sergt. put every day over my head, and for no earthly reason but that they wear a finer coat, gambol and play the fool, more kittenishble than I do."*[37]

Apparently Captain Chilton was not just bothered about promotions. He was also upset about all of the romantic competition he faced. He complained that, *"while they (his fellow officers) wear fine clothes they cut me out of all chance of a sweet-heart. Jersey women are fond of Notions as they call our jimmy-lads..."*[38]

And just to add salt to his wounded ego, Chilton concluded the letter by reporting that Colonel Marshall had just returned from a dinner at headquarters where,

> *"he has dined with the finest ladies in Jersey, feasting his eyes and his stomach. His eyes sparkle at the thought of it"*[39]

During this relatively quiet period General Washington puzzled over General Howe's plans. Reports from New York suggested that Howe's army was about to embark on ships. To where though, was anyone's guess. With a 7,000 man British army under General Burgoyne marching from Canada,

---

[37] John Chilton to William Pickett, 8 July, 1777 in <u>Tyler's Quarterly</u>, 125
[38] Ibid.
[39] Ibid. 126

it was possible that General Howe intended to link up and effectively sever New England from the other states. On the other hand, Howe could land his army in the South and do untold damage to the relatively undefended states there. The Chesapeake might also be his destination, effectively flanking Washington and taking Philadelphia before General Washington could re-position his army. All of these possibilities had to be considered. As a result, General Washington decided to stay in central New Jersey until Howe's intentions became clearer.

Chapter Four

"Our March Was a Forced One"

Tour of the Jerseys

On July 12th, with indications that Howe was heading up the Hudson River, Washington set the American army in motion. Over the next eleven days the 3rd Virginia made its way northward, marching seventeen miles on July 12th, fifteen miles on July 13th and eleven miles on July 14th.[1] They paused for four days near the New Jersey-New York border, due to rain, and then resumed their march north. On July 23rd they arrived in Chester, New York, staying there for just one day before turning around and heading south again. The reason for this sudden change in direction was a report that the British fleet was actually heading south. Still unsure of its ultimate destination, but realizing that his army might be dangerously out of position to intercept Howe's army, Washington commenced a forced march back towards Philadelphia.

Captain Chilton noted in his diary that they marched 23 miles on July 25th. They got a very early start on July 26th, striking the tents at 3:00 a.m. and marching eleven miles by 9:00 a.m. An incident that thoroughly rattled Chilton occurred before they even began that day's march. Recent orders had reminded officers that they were expected to attend roll call with their men. Captain Chilton noted in his diary that,

---

[1] Chilton Diary, 12-23 July, 1777 in <u>Tyler's Quarterly</u>, 284

"I had not seen my chest for near a week. I was consequently very dirty with a long beard. I had embraced this opporty. of shaving & shifting and was about ½ shaved at best. I saw the Men turn out and also saw Mr. Blackwell (Chilton's lieutenant) go to hear the Roll call. For this I was arrested."[2]

He was not the only officer arrested that morning. Captains Wallace and Powell and four subalterns were also arrested, and they were all outraged. Chilton noted that within fifteen minutes of the incident the officers' swords were returned to them. All but Chilton refused to accept them, however, because they felt wrongly accused and affronted. Although Chilton felt equally offended, he also realized that Colonel Marshall had been urged to be strict and that he was actually a very dependable officer. He thought it best to accept Marshall's gesture because to pursue a grievance would, *"end in a manner that would do neither party honour..."*[3] Chilton also realized that any resolution would have to wait until after the probable battle with the British and he was, *"averse to giving my command up to men of their choseg to command my Compy."*[4] He therefore, swallowed his aggrieved pride for the good of his men.

The army marched a total of 25 miles that day, and, despite a late start due to rain, they marched another 21 miles the next. Such hard marching in the summer heat (seventy miles in three days) took its toll on the men. Captain Chilton recorded the hardships that were endured in his diary.

"...we were ordered to sit down, in the Sun no water near, to refresh our selves no victuals to eat as the (march) of last night was so late that nothing could

---

[2] Chilton Diary, 26 July, 1777 in <u>Tyler's Quarterly</u>, 285
[3] Ibid.
[4] Ibid.

be cooked, no wagons allowed to carry our Cooking Utensils, the soldiers were obliged to carry their Kettles pans &c. in their hands, Clothes and provisions on their backs."[5]

The July heat made every step miserable and the men suffered greatly for want of shoes. Chilton continued,

"As our March was a forced one & the Season extremely warm the victuals became putrid by sweat & heat – the Men badly off for Shoes, many being entirely barefoot."[6]

At one stop in the march, the 3rd Virginia underwent an inspection to see what items could be discarded along the route.[7]

Fortunately for the men, the pace of the march soon slowed, with the regiment covering only 35 miles over the next three days. The 3rd Virginia arrived at the Delaware River on July 31st and experienced a mishap while crossing. One of the wagons carrying many of the regiment's tents, including Captain Chilton's, over-turned while being ferried across the river. Chilton noted in his diary that,

"I lost my Tent but luckily the Bed Clothes were wrapped up in Mr. Mountjoy's Tent, and the bulk kept the water from soaking through so they floated."[8] That night the 3rd regiment was, *"obliged to take to the woods for want of Tents."*[9]

---

[5] Chilton Diary, 27 July, 1777 In <u>Tyler's Quarterly</u>, 286
[6] Ibid.
[7] Ibid.
[8] Chilton Diary, 31 July, 1777 in <u>Tyler's Quarterly</u>, 286
[9] Ibid.

For most of August the American army was stationed only a day's march outside Philadelphia. Once again, General Washington had a difficult time determining the intentions of General Howe. On two separate occasions, Washington concluded that Howe's naval movement to the south was actually a feint to draw the American army in that direction. However, each time he prepared to march north, news arrived that the British fleet was still sailing south. Unbeknownst to Washington, the British encountered contrary winds, and their voyage took far longer than anticipated. The delay in reaching their destination caused General Washington great confusion and uncertainty. Although he still felt that Howe would attempt to join General Burgoyne in New York, the repeated sightings of the fleet heading south caused Washington to keep his army in Pennsylvania until he could definitively determine Howe's destination.

After the long marches back and forth across New Jersey, the American army welcomed the opportunity to rest. And for most of August that is what they did. During this relatively quiet period, Captain Chilton penned letters to his sister-in-law and brother. The first letter, dated August 14th to Betsy Chilton, was completely devoted to family matters. He expressed his deep gratitude for the care of his children.

> *"I have certain belief in my children being in best hands, it makes the fatigues of the campaign pass off as recreations. Who would not fight, bleed, even dare to die for such valuable friends! My task is an easy one compared to yours..."*[10]

Chilton was concerned that the task of raising two families was too great for her alone, and he once again asked that she hire someone to help.

---

[10] John Chilton to Betsy Chilton, 14 August, 1777 in <u>Tyler's Quarterly</u>, 128

"Do pray hire some good girl to assist you. I will gladly pay the hire. You impair your health by acting thus above your strength."[11]

He then mentioned his children by name and admitted that he could barely remember what they looked like. *"They will all be little strangers when the happiness of seeing them is granted to me."*[12]   Chilton added that he was glad to hear that there had been, *"an alteration for the better in Lucy."*[13]   His daughter had apparently gone through a rebellious stage during his absence but had lately calmed down. He confessed that Lucy's,

"...dear Mamma, when young, it is said, was wild, but when a grown woman, Virginia (which in my opinion excels in fine women) could not boast of a more valuable one."[14]

Chilton went on to say that he was pleased with the progress of Tommy's schooling. Joe, on the other hand, was reminded to, *"be a good boy and mind his books and he won't be beaten, his uncles will take care of that."*[15]   Apparently Joe's tutor, who Captain Chilton referred to as a tyrant, was very harsh. Chilton's brother, Charles, soon removed him from that situation, much to the relief of young Joe and his father.

Chilton's last known letter, to his brother Charles on August 17th, focused on the army. He wrote that he got along well with the Generals, some of whom thought that Chilton was overdue for a promotion. There was, however, an incident with General Adam Stephens, the Division commander, in

[11] Ibid.
[12] Ibid.
[13] Ibid.
[14] Ibid.
[15] Ibid.

which Captain Chilton felt wronged. He was escorted to General Stephens for being out after retreat had sounded. As Chilton told it,

> *"I had just gone up to drink our friends health in grog, the retreat beat, I told the Adjt. to step down while I paid, which I was doing when a sergeant and file of men came and informed me we must go to the Genl."*[16]

Chilton angrily went with the sergeant and when asked by General Stephens why he was out, replied in a most heated way that, *"...all regulations allowed 5 minutes but that I had not taken 2..."*[17] Chilton admitted that he had, *"made a slip,"* but believed it to be, *"too trifling to be sent for in that way."*[18]

General Stephens apparently agreed. He asked Chilton's pardon and offered him some grog. Chilton refused and left in a foul mood. The next day, General Stephens made another overture to Captain Chilton, who determined that the General, *"seemed sorry for what he had done, so I thought it was best to be on good terms again."*[19]

The anger Chilton had for General Stephens paled to that which he held for the regiment's new Lieutenant Colonel, William Heth. Heth was much younger than Captain Chilton, had served with Daniel Morgan at Quebec, and again as a Major in Morgan's 11th Virginia Regiment. He joined the 3rd Virginia sometime in July. Chilton complained that,

> *"...we have one gentleman in our Regmt. a Col. Wm. Heth, who takes great things to himself. Heth does not lack sense but is imperious to the last degree. I*

---

[16] John Chilton to his Brother, 17 August, 1777 in <u>Tyler's Quarterly</u>, 131
[17] Ibid.
[18] Ibid.
[19] Ibid.

was never tired of the Service till he joined our Regmt...Heth has greatly the ascendancy over Marshall, (the 3rd Virginia's Colonel) which I could not have believed. Anything clever done in the Regt, Heth takes the credit for it, what is not well done is thrown on Marshall."[20]

Fortunately for Captain Chilton, he had someone to confide in, namely, Captain William Blackwell of the 11th Virginia.

"If Captain William Blackwell were not out I should be almost tempted to quit the Service," wrote Chilton. *"His tent and mine adjoin so that we are* always *together when not on duty."[21]*

The American army had been stationary for almost three weeks when General Washington once again began having doubts about Howe's plans. On August 21st, Washington called a Council of War at which it was decided that Howe was probably sailing to Charleston, South Carolina. The Council concluded that it would be unwise to follow him there because the long march would be injurious to the army. Furthermore, they could not possibly arrive in time to be of any service to the state. So the council recommended, and General Washington agreed, that it was time to march north and join the American force challenging General Burgoyne's army from Canada.[22] However, just as orders for the march north were being prepared, a new sighting of the British fleet placed it in a shocking position. General Howe was sailing up the Chesapeake Bay.

[20] Ibid.
[21] Ibid.
[22] John Reed, Campaign to Valley Forge, (Pioneer Press, 1965), 58-59

General Washington reacted immediately, ordering the army to march to Philadelphia. On August 23rd, with the army just five miles outside the capital, Washington issued orders,

> *"for every Man to have clean clothes ready for the Morning, the Arms to be Furbished & bright."*[23]

Early in the morning of August 24th, the army, with springs of green in their hats and polished muskets in their hands, marched through Philadelphia. Camp followers (wives, families, prostitutes), along with many of the supply wagons, were diverted around the city.[24] General Washington desired to make as favorable an impression as possible on the city's inhabitants and the two hour procession was partially successful in doing so. One observer, John Adams of Massachusetts, wrote to his wife Abigail that,

> *"we have an army well appointed between us and Mr. Howe...so that I feel as secure here as if I was I was at Braintree."*[25] However, he also noted that, *"our soldiers have not yet quite the air of soldiers. They don't step exactly in time. They don't hold up their heads quite erect, nor turn out their toes so exactly as they ought..."*[26]

General Washington kept the army moving south, towards Wilmington, Delaware. They marched fifteen miles on August 25th, heading towards the British who, after a long and draining voyage at sea, finally disembarked near Head of Elk, Maryland. The thought of encountering the British army apparently did not concern Captain Chilton for his diary entry

---

[23] General Orders for 24 August, 1777 (The George Washington Papers at the Library of Congress : Online)
[24] Reed, 79
[25] Ward. 96
[26] Ibid. 97

on this date focused on the land and people of Delaware. He reported that the land and ladies were better here than up north.

> "...*the inhabitants too, have not that griping importunate countence as they have up in the N. westward, especially the Ladies, whose features are more soft, and they also have sound teeth.*" He also noted that, *They don't work so hard as the Virginians. They make as much Money but they do not live half so elegantly...*"[27]

The next two days were relatively quiet. On August 28th, as the Americans moved a bit closer to the enemy, Captain Chilton took the time to comment in his diary about the local girls. "*here we saw some fine Girls not much unlike our first Virga. Nymphs.*"[28] He had more pressing responsibilities to consider that day, however, as he was appointed the captain of the rearguard. Little of consequence occurred on Chilton's watch and that night, after being relieved from the guard, Chilton's company rejoined the regiment. They spent the night in the woods without tents.

The two armies were now very close to each other and General Washington made preparations for battle. He ordered that,

> "*A corps of Light Infantry is to be formed, to consist of one Field Officer, two Captains, six subalterns, eight Serjeants and 100 Rank and File from each brigade.*"[29]

---

[27] Chilton Diary, 25 August, 1777 in <u>Tyler's Quarterly</u>, 287

[28] Chilton Diary, 28 August, 1777 in <u>Tyler's Quarterly</u>, 287

[29] Additional After Orders to the General Orders for 28 August, 1777 (The George Washington Papers at the Library of Congress: Online)

Members of the 3rd Virginia, including Lt. Col. Heth, were attached to this Corps, which was commanded by General William Maxwell of New Jersey. On August 30th, Maxwell's corps was ordered forward to the vicinity of Cooch's Bridge, a likely route for the enemy. General Washington instructed Maxwell to place some of his men at the pass on the road and annoy the enemy should they attempt to march through. He added that the men should lie quiet and expect the enemy to move early in the morning.[30]

---

[30] George Washington to William Maxwell, 30 August, 1777

New Jersey

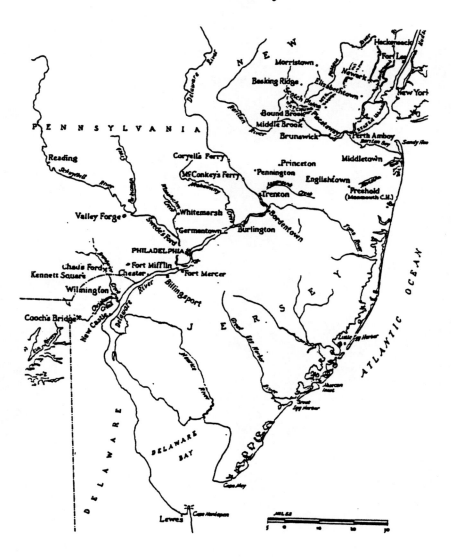

Chapter Five

"They Received the Enemy With a Firmness That Will Do Them Honor"

At Head of Elk, the British continued unloading their ships. It had been a long and grueling voyage for the army and they required a few days rest to recover from it. As a result, the days immediately following Howe's landing were relatively quiet. On August 31st, Captain Chilton noted in his diary that Lt. Col. Heth returned to camp for provisions.[1] Heth, along with Captain Ashby and Lt. Peyton, of the 3rd regiment, returned to Maxwell's light corps on September 2nd.

The enemy finally advanced towards the American army the next day. Maxwell's men, stationed over a mile in advance of Cooch's bridge, lay in ambush alongside the road. When the van of the enemy approached, around 9:00 a.m., a running battle ensued. The Americans kept up an irregular fire for nearly two miles. By early afternoon, however, the relentless pressure of the enemy forced Maxwell to disengage and retreat toward the main American force. His men had done their job, delaying the enemy for a good part of the day, and providing an early warning to the rest of the American army.[2]

Captain Chilton's company had a much easier time of things that day. They spent a few hours at their alarm post and then returned to camp. The enemy seemed content with sweeping Maxwell's Light Corps aside and declined to push any closer to the American main line. Both sides established

---

[1] Chilton Diary, 31 August, 1777 in <u>Tyler's Quarterly</u>, 288
[2] Reed, 100

pickets and settled in for the night. On the night of September 4th, Captain Chilton commanded a 40 man picket guard along the Red Clay Creek. The enemy was reportedly nearby, but the night passed peacefully. In the morning, Lieutenant Colonel Febiger, of the 11th Virginia, arrived with 200 men and a number of axes to block the road with trees.[3]

Three days later, on September 7th, reports that the enemy had stripped itself of its excess baggage caused General Washington to issue similar orders. The tents and heavy baggage were sent to the rear. All signs pointed to a British push at any moment, and indeed, it soon came. Rather than a push through the American lines, however, Howe stole a march around the right flank of the American army. General Washington reacted quickly, putting his men in motion early in the morning of September 9th. He was determined to reposition the army to protect both his right flank and Philadelphia. Hurrying north, the American army took up new positions at Chadd's Ford, on the Brandywine Creek. Captain Chilton's last diary entry described the march,

> *"at 2 in the morning we had orders to march, took the road from Newport to Wilmington 2 Miles, then turned to almost North about 2 Ms more we then marched* (on a) *West course 10 Miles S.W. & crossed Brandywine Creek and encamped on the heights of the Creek."* [4]

---

[3] Chilton Diary, 28 August, 1777 in <u>Tyler's Quarterly</u>, 288
[4] Chilton Diary, 9 September, 1777 in <u>Tyler's Quarterly</u>, 289

Battle of Brandywine

The scene was now set for a significant clash, one that would cost the American army over 1,300 men and the 3rd Virginia a fine officer. The British commenced their attack early in the morning of September 11th. Their plan was for General Knyphausen, with nearly 7,000 men, to feint an attack along the American front at Chadd's Ford, while General Howe led a force of over 8,000 men on a march around the American right flank.[5]

Facing Knyphausen's force was General William Maxwell's 800 man Light Corps, who were once again stationed in advance of the main American line, a few miles west of the Brandywine. At 7:00 a.m. Maxwell's advance guard, commanded by Captain Charles Porterfield of the 11th Virginia regiment, hit the British advance with a well-aimed volley. Porterfield's instructions were to, "deliver his fire as soon as he should meet the van of the enemy and then fall back" a half a mile to the rear.[6] His company did precisely that, dropping a number of British soldiers, but not halting their march.

Porterfield's men retreated and reformed on the next American position, once again pouring a close and destructive fire on the British.[7] This fighting withdrawal went on all morning, with Maxwell's men using trees and stone walls for cover, and grudgingly yielding ground. Eventually, however, the force of the British attack was just too great for the American Light Corps to resist, and they crossed the Brandywine and re-joined the main American line.[8]

---

[5] Samuel Smith, The Battle of Brandywine, (Philip Freneau Press : Monmouth Beach, NJ, 1976), 9
[6] Ibid. 10
[7] Ibid.
[8] Reed, 120

The 3rd Virginia, as part of General Stephen's Division, was stationed a few miles above Chadd's Ford. They heard the morning fight draw closer and braced for the full force of a British attack. It never materialized, however, as Knyphausen halted at the Brandywine, seemingly content with having pushed the Americans across the creek.

At American headquarters, General Washington was suspicious. He received conflicting reports of an enemy column moving toward his right flank. When the first sighting of such a force arrived, Washington ordered Generals Stirling and Stephens to change their division fronts and march four miles to the Birmingham Meeting House. Soon however, a contradictory report on the enemy's whereabouts caused Washington to halt the re-deployment. For two hours the men of Stirling's and Stephen's divisions, including Captain John Chilton and his men, waited while General Washington tried to make sense of the conflicting reports.

By 2:00 p.m., Washington was finally convinced that the British were indeed moving against his vulnerable right flank. He ordered General Stirling and General Stephens to resume their march as quickly as possible. General Sullivan was ordered to re-deploy his division as well, and to assume command of the whole force. In essence, General Washington had refused, or bent, his entire right flank at a right angle to its original position. Stirling's and Stephen's men arrived at the hills near Birmingham Meeting House just ahead of the British assault and prepared to meet their attack.

Brigadier General Woodford's brigade deployed on a hill about one hundred yards southwest of the Birmingham Meetinghouse. They were positioned on the extreme right of the American line. This meant that their own right flank was uncovered. As a result, General Woodford sent the 170 men of the 3rd Virginia to occupy an orchard to the north of the Meetinghouse. Colonel Thomas Marshall's men were thus given the responsibility of covering the right flank of the entire line. The men crossed a deep vale and took position amongst the fruit trees. A mile to their front sat thousands of enemy troops, resting from their seventeen mile march.

The 3rd Virginia's position would later be known as Marshall's Wood, and according to General George Weedon, who would soon come upon the scene, the 3rd regiment,

> *"had orders to hold the wood as long as it was tenable & then retreat to the right of the brigade."*[9]

The 3rd Virginia's detached and vulnerable position became even more vulnerable when the entire American line was shifted to the right to allow General Sullivan's division to properly position itself on the American left. General Weedon noted that,

> *"In making this Alteration, unfavorable Ground, made it necessary for Woodford to move his Brigade 200 Paces back of the Line & threw Marshall's wood in his front."*[10]

The 3rd Virginia was now in front of the main American line. The men, long trained in linear tactics, must have felt very exposed and isolated in this position, yet they held their post.

The fighting at Birmingham began around 3:30 p.m. when the British advance guard, comprised of German jagers, British dragoons and light infantry, approached the 3rd Virginia in the orchard. According to a British officer, the advance guard, *"received the fire from about 200 men in an*

---

[9] Brigadier General George Weedon's Correspondence Account of the Battle of Brandywine, 11 September, 1777. The original manuscript letter is in the collections of the Chicago Historical Society. Transcribed by Bob McDonald, 2001.
[10] Ibid.
[11] Smith, 16

orchard."[11] This unexpected American resistance caused the to British take cover behind a fence, two hundred paces from Marshall's men.[12] Captain Johann Ewald, commanding the enemy advance force, noted that,

> *"About half past three I caught sight of some infantry and horsemen behind a village on a hill in the distance. I drew up at once and deployed...I reached the first houses of the village with the flankers of the jagers, and Lt. Hagen followed me with the horsemen. But unfortunately for us, the time this took favored the enemy and I received extremely heavy small-arms fire from the gardens and houses, through which, however, only two jagers were wounded. Everyone ran back, and I formed them again behind the fences or walls at a distance of two hundred paces from the village... "[13]*

General Weedon, noted that Colonel Marshall,

> *"...received the Enemy with a Firmness which will do Honor to him & his little Corps, as long as the 11th of Sepr. is remembered. He continued there ¾ of one Hour, & must have done amazing execution."[14]*

General Light Horse Harry Lee, writing about the battle years latter, concurred, noting that the 3rd Virginia,

---

[12] Ibid. 17
[13] Captain Johann Ewald, <u>Diary of the American War: A Hessian Journal</u>, (New Haven & London: Yale Univ. Press, 1979), 84-85 Translated & edited by Joseph P. Tustin.
[14] Weedon Correspondence, 11 September, 1777

"...bravely sustained itself against superior numbers, never yielding one inch of ground and expending thirty rounds a man, in forty-five minutes."[15]

Even the main British battleline, upon arriving at the advance guard's position, was forced to halt momentarily to seek cover. One British officer reported that the American fire was so intense that,

"the trees (were) cracking over ones head. The branches riven by the artillery, the leaves falling as in autumn by the grapeshot."[16]

The British eventually resumed the attack and their overwhelming numbers pushed the 3rd Virginia out of the orchard. Colonel Marshall re-positioned his men approximately one hundred paces to the rear, behind a stone wall at the Birmingham Meetinghouse. The 3rd Virginia maintained such a heavy fire from behind the wall that the attacking British forces were compelled to veer around the flanks of the Virginians.[17]

The situation on the left side of the American line was much different. General Sullivan's division had barely arrived when they were struck by the enemy. In a very short time most of Sullivan's division retreated in disarray. The two remaining American divisions, Stirling's and Stephen's, attempted to hold their ground, but British pressure was too great. Fearing that the 3rd Virginia was about to be surrounded, Woodford ordered its withdrawal, and it joined the brigade in a general retreat.[18] The fight resumed on a

---

[15] Henry Lee, <u>The Revolutionary War Memoirs of General Henry Lee</u>, (New York: Da Capo Press, Originally Published in 1812), 89-90
[16] Smith, 17
[17] Ibid. 18
[18] Weedon Correspondence, 11 September, 1777

second hill, a half mile in the rear, but again the Americans were forced back. Fortunately, General Greene's division, marching four miles in 40 minutes, arrived in time to provide cover for the retreating Americans. The British ended their pursuit at sunset, in possession of the field, and victory. American losses in killed, wounded, and captured, were approximately 1300, more than double the roughly 600 casualties of the British.[19]

Twenty one year old Joseph Townsend, a resident of the area, witnessed the battle from a nearby hill. When the fighting subsided, he walked to the Birmingham Meeting House to see the results. According to Townsend,

"We remained on the hill (Osborn's) *for some time, and when the engagement appeared to be nearly over...I proposed to some of my companions that we should go over to the field of battle and take a view of the dead and wounded...We hastened thither and awful was the scene to behold – such a number of fellow beings lying together severely wounded, and some mortally – a few dead, but a small proportion of them considering the immense quantity of powder and ball that had been discharged. It was now time for the surgeons to exert themselves, and* (many) *of them were busily employed. Some of the doors of the meeting house were torn off and the wounded carried thereon into the house to be occupied for an hospital."[20]*

66

---

[19] Reed, 140
[20] Joseph Townsend, "Some Account of the British Army under the Command of General Howe, and of the Battle of Brandywine", in <u>Eyewitness Accounts of the American Revolution,</u> (Arno Press, 1969), 25-26 This was originally printed in 1846 in Philadelphia.

The 3rd Virginia suffered greatly in the battle, losing almost one third of its force. Regimental Surgeon David Griffith reported that over forty men and seven officers were killed or wounded.[21]

Captain Chilton

Sadly, Captain John Chilton was among the dead, mortally wounded in the fight for Marshall's Wood. The Virginia Gazette reported a few weeks after the battle that although Chilton was seriously wounded in the fight, he refused assistance. Instead, he imitated the bravery of British General James Wolfe, the hero of Quebec, by inquiring about the success of the day as he expired.[22]

Such behavior was completely in character for a man who cared so deeply for his men and his country. For eighteen months Captain Chilton had looked after his men's well being. He bragged about his boys in letters home, and lamented their suffering in winter quarters near Morristown. While other officers left camp to find more comfortable quarters in adjoining towns, or returned to Virginia on furlough, Captain Chilton stayed with his men. He even used his own money to purchase necessities for them. And during all this, he constantly worried about his family back home.

All of John Chilton's worries ended on September 11th, 1777 at Brandywine. With little ceremony, he was put to rest in an unmarked grave somewhere in Pennsylvania. But the survivors of the 3rd Virginia, battered and bruised like the American army as a whole, carried on. In fact, the army's morale was surprisingly high. They had lost the battle, it was true, but there was still plenty of fight left in them.

---

[21] Russell and Gott, 205
[22] Virginia Gazette, October 3, 1777, Williamsburg, Printed by Dixon & Hunter in Tyler's Quarterly, 133

Battle of Brandywine

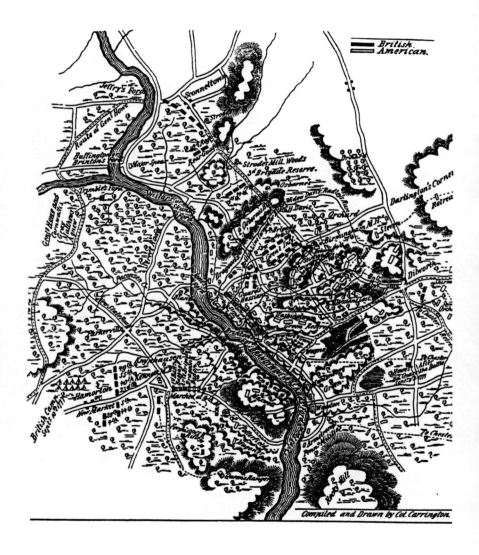

Compiled and Drawn by Col. Carrington.

Fighting at Birmingham Heights

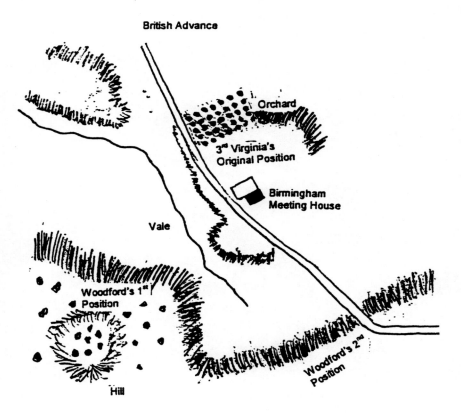

Chapter Six

Germantown to Valley Forge

The weeks following Brandywine were very difficult for the American army. Most of their baggage, including the tents, had been sent to the rear before the battle. It was almost a month before the men were finally re-united with them. As a result, they were constantly exposed to the elements. Furthermore, in an effort to counteract British troop movements toward Philadelphia, Washington's army marched over 100 miles on muddy roads, crossing the Schuylkill River three different times.[1] Despite Washington's efforts, however, the British maneuvered the Americans out of position and marched into Philadelphia unopposed on September 26th, 1777. General Howe immediately began fortifying the city in preparation for winter quarters. In doing so, he divided his force and presented General Washington with an opportunity for redemption.

Battle of Germantown

General Washington's plan was bold and complex. Early in the morning of October 4th, four American columns would hit the British advance guard, stationed just north of Philadelphia in the village of Germantown,. If everything went according to plan, the Americans would strike the surprised British with overwhelming force from four locations. Coordinating such an attack however, proved difficult. The four columns, numbering 12,000 men, marched

---

[1] Thomas McGuire, <u>The Surprise of Germantown: October 4th, 1777</u> (Cliveden of the national Trust for Historic Preservation, 1994) 3

all night to reach their proper positions, covering between 14 to 20 miles depending on their assigned route.[2] They struck at daybreak, catching the British by surprise and driving them towards Philadelphia. General Woodford's brigade, temporarily commanded by the 3rd Virginia's Colonel Thomas Marshall, was on the extreme right of General Greene's column. They arrived at Germantown nearly forty minutes late, with the other American columns already heavily engaged.[3] As Greene's division continued its advance, heavy cannon and musket fire to the right, drew Woodford's brigade in that direction.[4] The brigade was soon completely separated from General Greene's division, and drawn instead, toward a battle for control of Benjamin Chew's stone mansion.

Although the American army had already swept most of the British past the Chew mansion, over 100 soldiers of the 40th regiment barricaded themselves inside the building.[5] Its thick stone walls protected the British from much of the American fire. Nevertheless, the rebels were determined to take the house. As a result, a bloody struggle ensued, and the 3rd Virginia, along with the rest of Woodford's brigade, headed straight for it.

When they arrived at the mansion, they joined the Americans already there in trying to storm the building. The battle was intense and the noise drew the attention of Pennsylvania troops under General Anthony Wayne who had already advanced several hundred yards past the house. Fearing that the British had somehow launched a counter-attack in their rear, they about faced and marched toward the Chew house to investigate.[6] The morning fog and smoke of battle reduced visibility around the mansion to near zero. Woodford's troops suddenly saw a battle line advancing

---

[2] Ibid. 32
[3] Ibid. 75
[4] Ibid. 76
[5] Ibid. 49
[6] Ibid. 79

toward them. Assuming that it was the enemy, the Virginians fired a volley into its ranks. The startled Pennsylvanians returned fire. It is unknown how long the mistaken exchange of fire lasted, but it created enough damage and confusion to help undermine the American advance.[7]

The British soon rallied and pushed the now confused Americans back in some disorder. The British, however, were battered themselves and did not aggressively pursue. This allowed the American army to retreat in relative order. Although the 3rd Virginia suffered few casualties, the Virginia Line, as a whole, had 30 men killed, 117 wounded and 181 missing. Total American losses were estimated at over 1,000 men. Once again victory eluded the Americans, but just barely.

For the next two months the American army encamped just a few miles outside Philadelphia, too weak to dislodge the British, yet still a threat to their foraging parties. Although the losses at Brandywine and Germantown dampened American spirits, news of the victory at Saratoga dramatically boosted morale. This undoubtedly helped General Washington's army survive the challenges to come at Valley Forge.

---

[7] Ibid. 81

Battle of Germantown

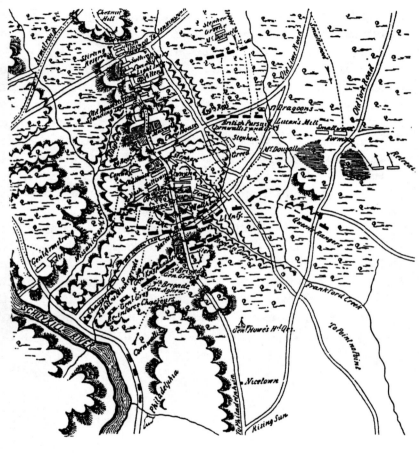

Compiled and Drawn by Col. Carrington.

American
British Original Position
British Advance.

1000 Yards.

Valley Forge

As winter approached, the American army remained encamped north of Philadelphia, in the village of Whitemarsh . Congress urged General Washington to attack and drive the British from the capital and he hoped to oblige them. But the American commander eventually realized that his army was just too weak and exhausted. As a result, Washington ended the campaign and established a winter encampment at Valley Forge. The army arrived there on December 19, 1777 and immediately began constructing huts for the winter. The men had spent the last two months, with declining temperatures, in tents, or worse, out in the open, and they were in desperate need of better shelter. The 3rd Virginia, still assigned to Woodford's brigade, camped near the far right of the outer line of the encampment. Their alarm post, however, was to defend the interior line of works.

A January 1st, 1778 report on the arrangement of the army showed the 3rd Virginia regiment with 285 men on its rolls, but it is doubtful that anywhere near that many were present and fit for duty.[8] Those who did endure the hardships at Valley Forge scrambled to complete their twelve man huts before winter turned severe. They suffered through the endless shortages of food and clothing as well as the rampant illness that swept the camp. However, most of the 3rd Virginia was fortunate in one regard: their two year enlistments were due to expire that winter. In an effort to encourage the men to re-enlist, furloughs were offered in December. Over one third of the regiment took the furloughs and re-enlisted, 34 men joining the light dragoons and 54 men re-enlisting in the

---

[8] Arrangement of the Army for the Campaign 1778, January 1, 1778 (The George Washington Papers at the Library of Congress: Online)

regiment itself.[9] These men were given permission to return home until the spring. However, those who refused to re-enlist had to stay with the regiment until their enlistment actually expired. Even these men, though, departed before spring, leaving the 3rd Virginia a mere shell of itself. Only eighteen men were listed as present and fit for duty in March.[10]

The 3rd Virginia was the first regiment of Virginians to join Washington's army in 1776. They participated in the decisive battles of Harlem Heights, Trenton, Brandywine, Germantown, and the encampments at Morristown and Valley Forge. The regiment left Virginia with over 600 men and had a mere handful when spring arrived at Valley Forge. Some of Virginia's finest men, including Hugh Mercer, George Weedon, William Washington, James Monroe, and finally, John Chilton, served in its ranks.

Now it was time for others to step forward and replenish the regiment. It was time for others to take up the musket and join General Washington at Valley Forge. It was time for others to pay the ultimate price for freedom. The original members of the 3rd Virginia had already paid their share on the battlefields and in the camps and hospitals of the north. It was now time for other Virginians to do their part.

---

[9] Return of Those Noncommissioned Officers and Privates in the Virginia Line Whose Terms of Service Have Expired. February 24, 1778 (The Washington Papers at the Lib. of Congress: Online)
[10] Charles H. Lesser, ed. The Sinews of Independence: Monthly Strength Reports of the Continental Army, (Chicago: Univ. of Chicago Press, 1976), 60

Valley Forge Encampment

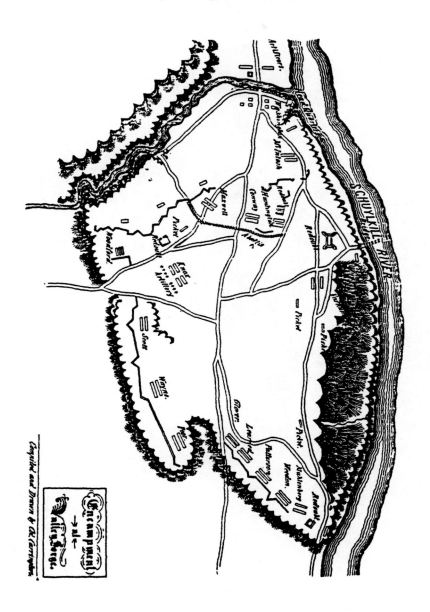

Appendix One

The Letters of Captain John Chilton

John Chilton to Joseph Blackwell
Sept. 13th, 1776

Dear Sir,

On our marches up and into the country, I have not thought it worth writing to you as nothing of moment have happened. At the end of the Fatiguing one we have had I embrace the opportunity of informing you, our Regiment have reached this place in good spirits and generally speaking healthy, tho not quite full, however; great joy was expressed at our arrival and great things expected from the Virginians, and of consequence we must go through great fatigue and danger. We lie in sight of the enemy's encampments who have got possession of Long Island and can see the belches of fire from their cannon at every discharge. We every hour expect to be in action but whether from the enemy's attacking us or we them, is uncertain as orders from head quarters are never known but when to be executed. We are stationed about 14 miles from New York near Kings Bridge which is above the place called Hellgate rather on the New England or Connecticut side of N. York. We are entirely surrounded with water, a rough sketch you will see on the back of this a very imperfect one; however you may get some notion of our situation from it. If the enemy should prove strongest, our post will not be a desirable one, (but to) succeed we must make the best of it. I write in a hurry in the confusion & noise of a camp and the thundering of cannon I fear it will scarcely be intelligible. I hope in my next to have more time and to give you a good account of the bustle of the times.

Johnny Blackwell would have wrote but just as he was getting ready for it was ordered upon guard, Joseph we left behind sick with fever and ague but hear he is coming up recovered with Capt. West's Compy. from Loudoun who are daily expected in.

Johnny joins me & I know Joseph would were he here, in our compliments to yourself & Mrs. Blackwell and to all your Friends for they are ours and to ours for they are yours. I can't particularise and hope my friends will excuse me. Dicky Beale would write but has not an opportunity, he is well a fine little soldier, remember him to his mother and all his friends as a worthy lad whom I much esteem.------ I have this moment heard that the Council of War which set yesterday have determined to keep New York which we had some expectation of abandoning as it lies immediately under the shipping. God grant our endeavours will prove successful and you, yours and our mutual friends, all happiness is the Prayer of your obligated and grateful servt.

John Chilton

Captain John Chilton to Maj. Martin Pickett,
Mr. Thomas Keith, or Mr. Charles Chilton
Morris Height Camp
Sept. 17ᵗʰ, 1776

My dear Friends,

    I embrace the opportunity of writing to you by Sergt.
Beaver of Capt. West's Co. whose place Jacob Jessop has
taken. My epistle will be incoherent, scarcely to be
understood, but your partiality in my favor I know will make
anything from me pleasing, where the news it contains is not
too bad. I have nothing but the news of the camp to give you
and that which I have myself seen, There being so many
generals and field officers here that a Captain is only of
consequence in his own Company or Regiment, at most. I will
endeavor to state plain matters of fact, as they have appeared
to me.
    On Friday last the enemy's cannon played the greater part
of the day from their Forts shipping. Friday night we
discovered (that) a body of the enemy were landing on a small
island in the East River. Our Regt. were ordered to march at 3
o'clock in the morning, after marching and counter marching
till about 7 we returned to our camps. Saturday, about
midnight we were ordered out and paraded as the day before,
returned to Camp, Sunday we had scarce time to get our
breakfast after returning, being informed of the enemy's
having taken possession on N. York and our Troops, who
were chiefly from Connecticut, having shamefully abandoned
their Posts below us without exchanging a fire. Our soldiers
were greatly exasperated and being drawn up for Battle, it was
very discoverable that they were determined to fight to the last
for their country; every soldier encouraging and animating his
fellow. This night our Regt. were on guard posted on an
eminence over against the enemy. Monday morning we

marched down toward them and posted ourselves near a meadow having that in our front. No. River to our right, a body of woods in our rear and on our left, we discovered the enemy peeping from their Heights over their fencings and rocks and running backwards and forwards. We did not alter our positions. I believe they expected we should have ascended the hill to them, but finding us still, they imputed it to fear and came down skipping towards us in small parties. At the distance of about 250 or 300 yards they began their fire. Our orders were not to fire till they came near but a young officer (of whom we have too many) on the right fired and it was taken up from right to left. We made about 4 fires. I had fired twice and loaded again, determined to keep for a better chance, but Col. Weedon calling to keep our fire (he meant for us to reserve it but we misunderstood him) I fired once more. We then wiped and loaded and sat down in our ranks and let the enemy fire on us near an hour. Our men observed the best order, not quitting their ranks tho exposed to a constant warm fire. I can't say enough in their favour, they behaved like soldiers who fought from principle alone. During this, 3 companies of Rifle-men from our Regt. West's, Thornton's and Ashby's, with other Companys of Riflemen were flanking the enemy and began a brisk fire on the right of them, on this they began to retreat up the hill carrying off their dead and wounded − for we had galled them a little −And then, let me not forget the brave Marylanders who were below us and sustained the hottest of the fire and must have done the greatest execution as they kept a constant fire after we were ordered to reserve ours. The Enemy retreated about a quarter and a half when they were re-enforced by men and cannon. We had but one field piece in the battle and they had several. The Battle began between 8 and 9 in the morning and lasted till about 2. It was rather a skirmish than a battle. However, it has taught our enemy that we are not all Connecticut men and they seem more peaceably inclined than before. Their task was to have marched through our Camp to King's Bridge,

4 miles above us the day of the Battle. But they are deceived for once and I hope will ever so when they assign themselves such tasks. We had three killed & wounded in our Regt. You don't know any of them. Major Leitch was also wounded badly, he received 3 balls, one just above his groin, the other two just above the groin in the side of his belly. He is a man of spirit and bears it as such, it is very dangerous, but I hope not fatal. There were about as many more in other Regmts. killed and wounded. We lost a Colonel, I don't know his name, one Nolton, a fine man, one of the New England men. It is said we killed a field officers of theirs and about 50 privates. From the blood and bustle they made carrying off the killed and wounded they certainly had many more killed than we had. You will see a better acct. in the papers.

Johnny Blackwell joins me in our sincerest wishes for your families and all Friends and hope you will esteem us.

Your, loving friend,

John Chilton

P.S. Tell the old Planters in Fauqr. their sons are fine fellows and soldiers.

P.S.S. Since I finished my letter am informed that we had 20 killed and as many wounded. It is said that the enemy consisted of about 10,000. Tho, suppose they had not more than about 2 or 3,000 in the field, we had not so many. We have formed a line from River to River, which is about a mile and a half.

I wrote my last of the 13th inst. to Mr. Blackwell which I hope will get to his hand.

Captain John Chilton to Friends
Camp at Morris Heights
October 4th, 1776

My dear Friends,

I sat down the other day and wrote you a long, tedious epistle with very little in it and finding that Major Williams intended staying a little while with us, thought by leaving it open if anything happened to inform you of it, but it mislaid for which you won't be sorry as I haven't time to be so prolix now, It chiefly consisted in congratulations to yourselves and our friends in Fauquier, also to all inquiring friends.

Since the skirmish of the 16th of Sept. the Enemy have been peaceable but seem vastly busy and we expect something every hour. We are on our guard and our men seem resolutely bent to give them a warm reception at the meeting. The Yankees, who were timorous when we first came here, have plucked up a heart and I hope will fight lustily. There were 3 ships and a Tender lying opposite the Enemies' Camp about a mile below our lowest lines, within these 2 days two more and a Tender have joined them. What or when they intend to attack is uncertain. I hope we may be ever ready to receive their attacks as men fighting for Liberty should do. The brave Major Leitch who died of his wounds received the 16th was interred yesterday by the side of Major Henly, who bravely fell some days ago in attempting to take Montezures, a small island in East River. His Men were not true to him who were in other boats and did not land, when that gallant officer and 15 or 16 men were cut off. However, the boat got off and the remainder escaped. Our men have been sickly with Fevers and agues but are now mending – we have plenty of good beef, but no variety of other food, and tho we are between two rivers we get no fish and very few oysters or clams or cockles. The oysters are good, sell by the 100. We sometimes get Pork and Pease, Rum, Brandy &c., at 16 (It has sold at 32).

You see we have no news, imagine you've had different accounts of men killed and wounded on the 16th of last month. Nor are we certain as to how many of our own side were killed. The Army is so large there is no knowing the exact number, but it is computed we had 50 or 100 killed and wounded. The Enemy about 300, if their deserters say the truth. One of which at least was a Field Officer.

One side of the field of Battle is a steep Rock precipice where we imagine they threw many of their dead as the buzzards and ravens resort to that place constantly.

I wish to hear from you a circumstantial account of your domestic affairs, your health, the budding genius of your little ones and mine. Crops of corn, if good, Beef, pork &c plenty. My brother Charles, you know the Beef, Pork, etc. on my place are yours, use them, my brother. Make my overseer take care of Fanny's colt, if I am spared to return he may be serviceable to me. Tell the Fathers of my brave boys their sons are soldiers. Give their and my love to them. Remember me by the first opportunity to my brother Thomas and sister Steerman and all my Westmoreland friends.

You see I can't sit down without writing a deal to little purpose, but your goodness will excuse a man near 500 miles distant if he is a little prolix in writing to such dear friends.

Adieu my dear Friends, may the Preserver of all things keep you and permit me to return as you would wish to see a soldier engaged in this glorious cause and who flatters himself that he is in your esteem would wish himself to present you.

John Chilton

P.S. Tell old Feggs I han't forgot him or any of my people.

Oct. 6th, We have just removed from our old encampment about ½ mile into the wood where we are building like Moonacks in the ground, nothing has yet happened. We send out scouting parties for the plank we want for our hovels, cabbages, apples &c.   I begin to think that mankind when engaged in warfare are as wary and timorous of each other as deer are of men, and the boldness of one party increases as they find the other fearful.   After the battle we were very cautious of encroaching too far on the Enemy's sentinels, but we have, as it were by stealth, pushed them from one post to another until they have hardly ground to stand on without their fortifications. An attachment of 100 men under Genl. Putnam (of Virginians) went last night and foraged in the teeth of the Enemy who chose to let them take all they wanted without being so ill natured as to give one fire.

   Messrys Keith & Chilton, If wheat sells low would it not be a good scheme to have it spiritualized & make money of it that way, except a barrel or so, which I would have double stilled to put up and get age, and if I have the happiness to come home free, we may have the pleasure of enjoying ourselves over a good bowl of it. If I should not come home there will be the more for you. It will not be the worse for age, but this I leave to your better judgment.

   I've directed this to Major Pickett and you but suppose before this reaches Fauqr. he will be at convention like a worthy member. Mrs. Pickett will probably be pleased to see in what manner I write from our Dens, so it will answer the same purpose as if the Major read it himself. The Jersey men don't seem to approve of our way of building, their being no up-chambers to our houses. There came over a deserter to us this morning from the Enemy and our scouts made two prisoners. We must fight soon, the Ministerials pride will be roused at many of these impertinences.

Joe and John Blackwell join me in everything affectionate to you and all friends. Joe has been sick and sullen as you can imagine, he has mended so as to go on duty but he is not so merry disposed as your neighbor Hookie.

God bless you all.

John Chilton

Captain John Chilton to his brother, Charles Chilton
Brunswick, New Jersey
Nov. 30th, 1776

Dear Brother,

I wrote from this place by Captain Ashby at which time I expected to have been in Winter Quarters before this. The day after his departure we were ordered up to Elizabeth Town about 20 miles hearing the Enemy had crossed No. River and got to a small town, called Hackensack; by the time we got there they had proceeded to Aquakinac Bridge, 4 or 5 miles nearer. 26th they crossed Aquakinac River above (the) Bridge by fording it. Our men were mostly at Newark and made no opposition. 27th, all the forces came through Elizabeth on their way to Brunswick. Our Regmt. brought up the rear. This was a melancholy day, deep miry road and so many men to tread it made it very disagreeable marching, we came 8 or 10 miles and encamped. Yesterday, we reached this place. How long we shall stay, I can't say, but expect we shall make a stand near this place if not at it, but no certainty when the Enemy are advancing on and an engagement may happen before tomorrow night. We must fight to a disadvantage.

They exceed us in numbers greatly. You will wonder what has become of the good army of Americans you were told we had. I really can't tell, they were in some degree imaginary. Militia, some enlisted for 2 some 4, some 5 months, their times were mostly out before the battle of the White Plains,--if I may call it a battle – and I suspect that the thinness of our Troops was one reason we were not allowed to fight them that day. The same reason prevents us now, and until we get a reinforcement, but as I told you before I do not know where this stand will be. It is conjectured by some that Burgoyne, from Quebec, is to join Howe and make a push for Philadelphia, but this is not known. You may guess we are in some confusion, and yet let me tell you not so much as you may imagine. I've just heard the Enemy are making to cross this river about 8 miles above here. Upon certain intelligence we shall move up I suppose. O, god that our Congress should raise men just for an expense till time comes for them to fight and then their time be out! Howe must have known of this, there are so many Tories all over the Continent. The very time of his landing first was about the time of whole Regmts time being up. Genl. Lee is yet in N. York Govmt. with 10 or 12000 but fear he can't join us in time, and indeed, I don't know whether he should come to our assistance. If he should and we get them a little further in the Country we could shortly give a good account of ourselves and them too, I trust, but if the Militia joins us in a day or two, I hope they will repent their bold step. Our men are very willing to fight them on any terms but our generals are the best judges when it is best to be done.

The appointment of officers we have just received by Armistead's Mercenary, Maddux, which surprises us all. If men were to be particularly preferred for seeing service where was Isham Keith, John Blackwell and Joe who have seen more service in one month than he, the Capt. could see in Williamsburg in an age. Isham so old a soldier and so good a one. Don't think me partial when I say that Joe and John are in no way inferior to Isham. Poor Uncle Ishe is sick at Trenton, so is Captain Ashby. I have pretty well got over my jaundice and the Company are healthy except three or four, who are not dangerous I hope.

Thank you kindly for your favor by Maddux, but more particularly the trouble you take in my affairs. How shall I thank Betsy for the great pains she takes with my dear little ones in clothing them and my Negroes, she has more than she can do. It will kill her, so pray, my brother, get a good girl or a Negro wench and I will pay for hire and take anything from my plantation that you stand in need of. There are two good smart steers, get corn from my house and make Gafney fatten one or both for you. Use everything as your own. I should do it in your place, it is justice, which is expected, I may save a little, therefore, my dear brother pay off Harpy, Campbell, as nearly as you can. I don't know what I owe Major Pickett, not much I hope, pay him. I don't own any other debts. Capt. E. Edmonds and Willis Green have accts. against me but there must be a great settlement first.

Give my love and sincerest thanks to Betsy, tell her I expect to be at Philadelphia this winter where I can supply myself with clothes of every sort. She is too good and gives herself too much trouble about me.

I am dear Brother, Yrs.

John Chilton

Captain John Chilton to his brother Charles Chilton
Morristown, N. Jersey
Feb. 11, 1777

Dear Brother:

My last by Capt. Powell was addressed to Mrs. Blackwell which I expect you have seen. I should have written you by John Hall, but was summoned to Chatham, a small town about 7 miles from this, to inquire into the conduct of Col. Buckner, our countryman, who you have no doubt heard behaved in a manner unbecoming an American. Buckner was cashiered and rendered unfit for any military Post in the Continental Army forever. You will see an account of it in Purdie's paper more at large. There was but a single circumstance saved him from being shot. It will be to no purpose to inform you what this was unless you had heard the whole trial. Great is the scandal the Virginians sustained on this unmanly conduct of his, until the day of his trial when the gallant and not enough to be esteemed Col. Scott, of whom you have heard me speak, with 300 men was bravely standing out 1000 English who had two field pieces. All day we could hear the report of their cannon which they took care to fire at too great a distance for Scott to do them any harm, only by small scouting parties. They killed and wounded 3 of our men and began to retreat, they were followed by this handful to their very lines. We don't know their loss but it could not be much as we were not well prepared and could not venture too nigh their lines. The Col. had been very sick for some days before and was very unwell at the time of the engagement. This and another engagement he had with them about ten days before when he made the so much boasted English Grenadiers run with an inferior number, and they were backed by a number of Hessians and other forces, has a little wiped out the stain of Buckner or at least have silenced those gentlemen who were scoffing "What, can Virginians run too!" especially as a certain Northern Col. was to be arrested, I hear, for leaving Scott on his first engagement, for while he was pursuing the Grenadiers (I forbear yet to mention his name) a body of Hessians came on his rear whom at first he took to be friends, but Scott was not to be taken so, he made his escape and the English &c. made the best of their way to their lines. This Col. was too fearful to assist so gallant an officer whose loss would be much felt. I have given you some account of our bickerings here which are so common that it is no news to hear of them. Hardly a day passes that more or less shots are not exchanged and prisoners or deserters &c. coming in. I saw 4 Highlanders go up to headquarters about an hour ago, I can't say whether as prisoners or deserters.

Hall, I fear, will give you a discouraging account of the loss our Regmt. sustained. The middle of Dec. I brought all my men into Pennsylvania. It was then the most healthy camp in the Regmt. The weather was extremely cold and duty hard, when we encamped at Blue Mount, the men bare of clothes and to a man we all had a surfeit, it was Tom Randall's servant. Upon application I could not refuse them leave to get clear of it. I advised them to go into the country to good farmer's houses and anoint for it, but by some strange infatuation, though contrary to my orders as well as advice, they would immediately push for Philadelphia where death and every kind of disorder lay in ambush for them. First the smallpox, and yellow and spotted fever, jaundice, and several other ailments and I told them and warned them of them. I heard of their being sick, some dying who had gone before, and sent for those who were well enough to come up. Either they never got my orders or did not choose to leave a place that fate seemed to have ordained they should go to.

Joe and Isham sick, were not able to join till middle of Jan. The trouble of the whole camp devolved on me as well as that of Capt. Ashby's and as if that had not been enough, marched up to this place where every officer but one went off. Col. Weedon was appointed Adj. Genl. so that I had the trouble and care of the Regmt. which though small was equally troublesome in many respects as the whole. The Pay-master not making regular payments distresses me too, for though I had money enough for my own men, and to spare, (of those with me) yet I find it very inconvenient for all, and yet they look to me for cash on every exigency.

Indeed some of their Capts. have wrote to me to furnish their men with money, and they, at the same time are out at some town living in luxury or capering away to Virginia while I, many times, scarcely know where my next shirt is to be washed, and I can't see good soldiers want. This to me has been a dreadful Campaign, I pray God, I may never experience the like. The loss of my men gives me the greatest uneasiness. If I could have been with them to have seen them well used, I could bear it with greater resignation, but I know they must have suffered many wants, poor young fellows! I sometimes blame myself for not going to them, for I had leave. But what should I do. The poor lads who had shared every danger with me begged I would not leave them in the very face of the enemy. The soldiers of other companies also asked I should stay. My own pride, and let me say reason, also told me it was not the time to take pleasure so I left it to those who went to take care of my sick. I hope they have done this but I have not heard. I am told Isham lost 18 men. I forbear to mention them because I am not sure who they are, as soon as I get time I will inquire and get their clothes, cash, &c. and transmit them to their sorrowful friends.

Lieut. Alvin Mountjoy, Lieut. Jos. Blackwell, Ensign R. Peyton have been under a strict Regimen for the Smallpox for some days. We expected we had taken it from a man who broke out with it. We expect to get leave tomorrow to get inoculated in a day or two if no symptoms appear. Joseph, we thought, was taken with it on Sunday, he was unwell yesterday and very ill all this day and no symptoms appearing. The Doctor gave him oil just before night, it has worked him and he is easier. We shall see whether in a day or two if it is smallpox. We are well prepared for it I hope.

And now let me finish this long epistle by desiring you to present my compliments to all friends. My love to you, Betsy and our children. We are in light spirits and from concurring circumstances expect this will be the last severe campaign for some time, for from some late British captures, (and those considerable) we are informed the Ministry can get no more foreign assistance and all Europe is likely to be embroiled next summer.

Adieu, My Brother,
Yours affectionately,
John Chilton

I long to hear from you all. How does Gafney go on, or do you keep him yet? You see we are obliged to write with gunpowder as well as fight with it.

Captain John Chilton to Major Pickett
Hanover Township, N.J.
March 19, 1777

Dear Major:

   I thank you for your favour of the 6th of Feby. I had just got out of smallpox for which I had been inoculated and had it favorably, but our Brother Joseph was not so lucky, he had it pretty severely. The laurels that he was receiving when yours came were whelts and carbuncles on his nose and face. I don't know whether they are of the kind that will please Miss Beale, though I don't believe he will bring many home with him as they begin to disappear fast. Be this as it will, he is very sullen, occasioned by a weakness in one of his eyes that was infected by the smallpox though not to injure it. He does not write for this reason, but desires to be remembered to you, Mrs. Pickett and all inquiring friends as does also your Humble Servt. Before Joe had the smallpox he talked of going to see Mr. Isaac Eustace of Stafford, when he returned home. I dare not say that he did not talk feelingly of his daughter Nancy, but this under the rose. Poor John, I pity him, he is certainly a most unlucky fellow, courted so many and missed of all. I shall advise him to sue Cocky Lee for half his wife's portion for I am sure he intended to court her on his return. If I had received your letter before he went to Virginia I might have known that his success in recruiting would turn out badly for of all persons a disappointed man is the most unfit to enlist men. He is really a good officer but unlucky I fear.
   As I write from camp to camp you will expect news no doubt, but I assure you we are very barren of news except skirmishing every day or two where two or three Britons knocked up will do. Gen. Howe was out with a few light horsemen reconnoitering and had like to have fallen into our hands, his horse plunged into a mire which he was obliged to

quit and mount the horse of one of his guards and escaped narrowly. They could have killed him, but wanted to take him alive. We were obliged to be content with the guard and general's horse. Howe has made a fine hand of it, he is now as nearly in Gage's situation in Boston as can be. The *Conqueror* of America finds himself, after all, his great conquest, in possession of a string of land inhabited by half-starved Tories, of about 14 miles in length and one and a half in breadth, and but one way to make his escape and that is by way of Amboy. What will the ministerial party say when it comes to be known in England that this is their whole possession on the Continent, and what will Junius say when he comes to be properly informed of the rapidity of Howe's conquest in over-running two colonies as they pompously wrote home they had done. But what will they all say if Howe should be so fool hardly as to endeavor to keep possession of his mighty conquest six weeks longer when they hear that his Army is all cut off or made prisoners of war. This I trust will be the case should he stay, for as soon as inoculation is over and a few more Troops arrive I expect he will be closely invested, and I hope his retreat cut off.

They now scarce dare creep out of their lines and when they do forage a little our scouting parties precipitate them into their lines again, like hares before a hound. They have smallpox among them worse than we have, provisions scarce, beef in New York selling at 13 pence per pound, oak-wood selling at 5 and 6 pounds per cord.

Their lines are so extensive that duty is excessive hard on them which gives them great colds and throws them into Pleurisies &c. They begin to desert over to us as fast as possible. In the course of last week 30 deserters came in, many had come before. Every opportunity they come to us, so that they have to have a double guard of those they can best depend on. The one to keep us from falling on them, the other to keep their disaffected (of which we are told by those with us that there are numbers both British & Hessians) from running over to us. We are told that in N. York there is a number of Hessians, as well officers as soldiers, under guard for disaffection. One piece of news I have to tell you is that I greatly want to see Virginia and its inhabitants. No country yet like old Virginia! The women here from 16 years old have lost their teeth. You'll see them with a fine satin *Cardinal,* dreadful large cap flounced off with ribands that cover their faces quite to their eyes. The *cardinal* hides a bed-gown, not always the most neat and cleanly, a quilted petticoat, check apron and sometime half boots. There are some exceptions as to dress, I have seen some pretty genteel, but not like my county women after all. They are expensive in their dress, I mean the first rates, such as Captain's and even Major's ladys' dress as first described. Men and women are desperate people for news and spoon victuals. They don't live half as well as in Virginia, nor do they any where live so well—

Enough of this, Remember me to Mrs. Pickett and family, Aunt Pickett, old uncle Cook, Jos Nelson, Old Hookle, --and John, Jim and the two Becks,--and all friends who ask for me and esteem me.

Your Aff. Friend and Humble Servt.

John Chilton

P.S. Fine times with you. No opposition that you fear. You sit at your ease while the other poor fellows, sweat and stir about, three of them to no purpose –Moffatt will out-poll Charles, I am apprehensive.

Captain John Chilton to Mrs. Betty Chilton
& Mrs. Judith Keith
Date: Unknown... Probably March or April 1777

My much loved and Respected Sisters:

I gladly embrace every opportunity of writing to you and sincerely wish that my subjects could be pleasing to you as it is my desire they should be. I know you are all patriots and wish the welfare of your Country and therefore look for news in every letter which is a scarce article here, except camp news which rarely has the existence of an hour.

I obtained leave the last week to visit my acquaintances of Quibble Town (the Fauquier volunteers) which is the second application I ever made and I am now paying severely for it. I walked down in my boots, had a pimple on my instep which the boot bruised and my foot is so inflamed that it is with difficulty I can go about the house where I am stationed which is two miles from Chatham, so I can't speak of the small politics of the army.

On Thursday last Col. Hendricks was sent off with 100 Virginians on an expedition, the design of which is not known. It is said the enemy have landed at King's Ferry, up Hudson's River, it is supposed to forage, or some imagine with an intent to draw a good part of our army that way that they may either make a stroke here or escape out of Brunswick. Whichever their intention is I hope we shall be ready for them, and if they think of scattering us for an advantage, they are mistaken in their politics, for that is not our way of fighting.

The smallpox having disordered one of our brother Joseph's eyes, he was left at Hanover, where we were inoculated to take care of the soldiers who were not so forward as those of us who marched down here. I heard from him Thursday, he was getting strong and hearty but his eye still continued weak. The soldiers were all fit for duty, I must send up and find how they all are. Joseph has not kept his word with me. I have sent to inquire after him but he has forgot me or thinks it is not worth while to be inquiring after a hearty, great grog-drinker. I really want him down, for lame as I am and—

Turn over

I thought to have made this half sheet do for letter cover and all, but could not help, according to custom, scribbling too much—Col. Hendricks detachment went up to Fort Lee, I imagine to nab the Sentrys that used to be placed on this side of No. River but suppose the Tories had informed of his approach, none were found there. He is returned to Elizabeth 14 miles from this –The Enemy are much in motion, they are leaving Amboy, but what is intended I can't say, I hardly think they will make their push this way, they pretend their push is intended for Philadelphia, but I rather think they are casting about for an escape.

Mr. Mountjoy is also lame. I greatly want his assistance and he is an active and good soldier, which sort are soon missing.

In the house where I like there is an old women, like old Jenny Stewart, a sort of *Doctress,* she was the other night telling me of a kind of vegetative bead among them, that was very good for fits of the mother etc., and produced me a string which divided will make pretty and good. I purchased of her a string which divided will make a string a piece for you. I have seen the beads before but took them for some sort of shell. Young and old wear them here, I particularly recommend them to Mrs. Keith in case she should be troubled with anything like the Hysterics, as she used to be very easily scared at nothing. I think this amulet quite requisite for her. I have also sent some of the seed that have not been threaded to raise from. Plant them in a hill as you do cucumbers in rich grounds about 14 inches apart, setting a stick by each seed to know them for they come up like coarse grass or broom-corn and branch out greatly and produce a vast many. Tend it well, they are very good for children when cutting teeth. The small seed they call Lin-seed which if powdered and put in Rum or other spirits will kill the vermin by anointing the hair in an hour – you'll laugh at me here and say I had better keep it for the army where vermin are so prevalent. However upon inquiry, I find it Larkspur seed which as they are tied up in the same cloth may serve to decorate your gardens, they being a pretty flower. You see, I have given up all notions of writing to your men, as the language of this place is, because they don't write to me.

I will neglect no opportunity of writing to my friends and hope their goodness will excuse the barrenness of the subject. I never care on what subject they write me so I hear from them. Give my best respects to all and receive them yourselves. I am yours and each of your most aff. and humble Servt.

John Chilton

Captain John Chilton to his brother, Charles Chilton
June 29, 1777

Dear Brother,

I am at this time stationed with 30 men to guard this pass; came here last night. Mr. Blackwell's & my Company with me, except a few who stay in camp with the baggage, we are all hearty, few complaints being now in the Army of sickness, there is a small lax but it wears off quickly. Our station is a pretty agreeable one, only two miles from Camp where we can at any time run for any necessary that we want from that quarter. Then we have the advantage of getting milk, butter &c. which are scarce articles in Camp.

26th past, our camp was at Piscataway which place the Enemy had abandoned a few days before. Col. Morgan with the Rifle Regmt. was on the Mattuchin lines at the time and our main army had come down into the Plains. The Enemy unexpectedly stole a march in the night of the 25th and had nearly surrounded Morgan before he was aware of it. He with difficulty saved his men and baggage and after a retreat, rallied his men and sustained a heavy charge until reinforced by Major Genl. Ld. Stirling, who gave them so warm a reception that they were obliged to retreat so precipitately that it had like to have become a rout. But being strongly reinforced he was obliged to retreat with the loss of 2 pieces of Artillery.

Brigadier Genl. was on the left and had a severe engagement, but was obligated to retreat also. The Enemy pursued this advantage as far as the Scotch Plains, which place they left that night suddenly returned into Perth Amboy.

This was done in consequence of some steps his Excellency, George Washington was taking, and had they staid that night a general engagement would have ensued I think. There were but few Virginians except Morgan in this battle. I imagine the reason His Excellency did not allow the engagement to be general was from a step the Enemy took as if they intended to gain the heights that we had left and destroy our stores, this is pretty generally conjectured, whether right or wrong I can't say. But be it as it may we make it suffice us that he had his reasons for it. This was one of Howe's Masterpieces and the small advantage he paid dearly for in all probability. The ground where his slain lay, we did not see.

We have but few missing considering the engagement which began about sunrise and continued first in one place, then in another very hot until 11 o' clock. The troops he engaged were very good marksmen who had many good fires on them so that there must have been many killed and wounded. The whole British force was engaged on this occasion even the seamen were brought. Two thirds of our Army was not in action. I was in 4 miles of the engagement and heard it all. Judge of my condition during it—alternate hopes and fears as the firing seemed favorable or otherwise.

Just as the battle ended Col. Marshall received orders to leave Piscataway & march up by way of Bound Brooke. A party of the Enemy had advanced within two miles of us, about 2000, and had sat down to refresh themselves. We marched off with colors flying and drums beating which they hearing and expecting we were coming to attack them made the best of their way to Perth Amboy, since when they seem peaceably disposed and keep close. I am informed that Genl. Scott yesterday sent out to feel their pulse but they did not seem "fightish" as the Yankees say, so I suppose they think they have done great things; but I verily believe that if they had staid till next morning they must have done greater, or it would have gone hard with them.

I have given you an account of this battle as nearly as I can and though it may not be altogether as good as you may see in the papers, you believe that it is nearly the truth. I hope long before this reaches you the smallpox may no more be a terror to you, and that it will find you all well. Excuse me to Mr.

Blackwell for not writing to him at this time. Time and paper both being scarce.

Betsy I hope will also excuse me but she must not neglect writing. Tell the children I have some hopes of seeing them this fall, as there is some talk of our Regmt. being sent home in order to recruit and enlist the old soldiers again. Tis thought by this piece of indulgence they will enter the Service again (But keep this secret).

I wish you would get Gafney to take good care of my colt and get Daddy Rogers to supple him. If there is not good pasture let him run in some field, and if he gets fat make him keep so. You'll say I am always talking about the colt, but consider, if I live to get home and peace restored, I shall want a good horse to ride, and I am satisfied I shall not bring money enough to buy unless my lottery scheme turns out, for my wages barely support me. Butter ½ dollar per pound, mutton 10 pence and whiskey a dollar a quart. Rum 12/ the last of which are two articles I must have. I am like Mr. Bowman with his canteen. It is all the comfort I have in this place.

Present my compliments to Mrs. Picket, Mr. Keith, Mr. Staunton, Capt. Pickett, Capt. Randall, Capt. Morehead and their ladies, and to their sons and daughters and little ones. Now I had like to have forgot my cousin Cooke again, Tell him to let me know if his little Betsy is as pretty as she used to be, and give my love to him, his wife and little ones. To Mr. Saytoris family, Mr. Stewart and daughter, Mr. Hathaway and all friends. Let the fathers of my boys know that their sons are all well. My love to you all, I am

Your Aff. Brother,

John Chilton

P.S. Don't forget to remember me to Mr. Blackwell and his family and Sam and his wife. J.C.

My love to Sister Randell and family. Let her know that
Tommy and Teddy are well, and they are in the same brigade
with me and the next Regmt. to ours. I see them every day in
Camp. Tell Mrs. Tomlin not to cry any more about Billy, he's
a fine Soldier.

J.C.

Captain Chilton to Captain Wm. Pickett
Morris Town, July 8th 1777

Dear Sir:

Illy as you have treated me, I have taken pen in hand rather
to revenge myself by way of a persecuting epistle, than any
expectation of getting a word from you for it, or giving the
least satisfaction to you in the perusal of it. Here I am 300
miles away from home, under the mortifying circumstances of
being called "Old Chilton" by the whole Army and seeing
boys whom I would not have made Sergt. of put every day
over my head, and for no earthly reason but that they wear a
finer coat, gambol and play the fool, more kittenishble than I
do, and this is not all, while they wear fine clothes they cut me
out of all chance of a sweet-heart. These Jersey women are
fond of Notions as they call our jimmy-lads and scarfs, and
they like 'a nice jiffer man". And yet, poor things, what with
drinking tea (they are desperate people for tea) spoon victuals,
and eating hot buckwheat cakes, there is hardly one above 16
that have their fore-teeth, nay that has a foretooth.

Now had I a chance of coming to old Virginia I could resign these crooked women with pleasure, but, Carlton with 5 or 6,000 men has sat down before Ticonderoga and had the assurance last week to order Genl. Sinclair out for his Worship to take place –the honest Scot however, told him that he was supplied with both men and ammunition, and provisions, more men than he knew how to stow upon his lines, upon which Carlton drew up and made some discharges of cannon. But on some well directed 18 pounders winged with death being discharged from our Battery, he wisely withdrew with precipitation and considerable loss. Then here's Howe, with his banditti. Clinton too, has just arrived with ample and honorable proposals to settle the difference between us.
This I suppose it to gain time for more foreign Troops to be brought in.

Under all these circumstances you have never sent me a line, but sit home and eat Hen-turkeys in a pudding bag and say of me, as Anthony did of Lepidus –"Fool Chilton"— it is too much. Write me a good long letter about Humphrey Brook, C. Bell, Old Pike and Jonathon Wild – and present my compliments to Mrs. Pickett, Aunt Pickett, old Mr. Cooke, your Brother, Capt. Buckner and lady, and Jemmy Withers, don't forget Jemmy Withers and his good little woman.

Fresh intelligence, Col. Marshall has just come from Head-Quarters where he has dined with the finest ladies in Jersey, feasting his eyes and his stomach. His eyes sparkle at the thought of it--(**Undecipherable sentence**)

Adieu, and if you don't despise my correspondence write me as above directed, or as you please so you do write me.

Yours,

John Chilton

Captain John Chilton to his Sister
Camp at Cross Roads, Pa.
14 August, 1777

Dear Sister,

With thanks I received your double favor by Mr. Morrison,
you did yourself too much trouble for me. I know not how I
am to repay it. Gratitude is all I can pretend to at present.
You have more to do for your own family than you are able to
go through and however commendable industry is; yet a
tender constitution might also have its due weight and not be
exerted above its true capacity. You haven't a strong
constitution therefore should reserve rather than overburden it
with fatigue and care. The loss of your girl Kate, is an
addition to your fatigues. Do pray hire some good girl to
assist you. I will gladly pay the hire. You impair your health
by acting thus above your strength. I am exceedingly happy in
having our families getting on so well over the smallpox and
your continued health. I reckon George looks like Andrew
Buckman, with his great – white eyes, Charley, I have
forgot—and Nancy, Indeed I don't remember any of the
children but Jack and Lucy. I hardly think I should know
Tommy and Joe. I have no conception of their features. Lucy
Pickett and Martin's features are more particularly familiar to
me than any, Orrick too I remember but have no conception of
Sukie, except her eyes, and Billy. They will all be little
strangers when the happiness of seeing them is granted to me.
I am glad you discover an alteration for the better in Lucy, it
was what I greatly wished and indeed flattered myself with,
for dear Mamma, when young, it is said, was wild, but when a
grown woman, Virginia (which in my opinion excels in fine
women) could not boast a more valuable one. Mrs. Keith, too,
was a rattle when young, but I have the pleasure of frequently
hearing fine things said of her. Then why should I despair of
my Lucy, she has the same excellent pattern assisted by her

four excellent daughters, to teach her young flittering feet to tread the paths of prudence and virtue. She is too young yet to listen to the force of reason, example is the only necessary for such unformed unsusceptible minds which I am happy in being assured she has before her. I have certain belief in my children being in the best hands, it makes the fatigues of the campaign pass off as recreations. Who would not fight, bleed, even dare to die for such valuable friends! My task is an easy one compared to yours, only the many great obligations you all load me with leave the balance with you.

Please to tell Tommy I am much pleased with the character his Tutor gives him. Tell Joe I am sorry his Tyrant beat him so, but he must be a good boy and mind his book and he wont be beaten, his uncles will take care of that. But he must not presume so far on their protection as to be a naughty boy. Tis a pity my namesake has lost the advantage of this year's schooling but he will be a good boy and bring it up next year, I'll warrant him.

Give my love to all the children and if they'll be good, all the soldiers shall love them when they get home. I am glad Doctor Boyd is to marry Miss Brooke, she is a fine girl and I shall ever esteem the Doctor for his care and human usage of the sick and wounded at the G. Bridge. Some parts of his character, I confess, I am not enamoured with, but all have their foibles.

Phil Neale is indebted to a bad constitution for a wife it seems. I think Miss Diggs takes him on a sorry recommendation.

Your brother Joe is courting, instead of recruiting men. He forgets his renouncing all the girls when he had the smallpox. I guess Alvin Montjoy will tell of it and blow Joe up, he said he would. I can't help being sorry for poor Capt. Scott's affliction of mind and body, both are too much to be borne. I once had a tender friendship for him, though I confess he had used me in a manner that had cooled it much, long before I entered the service, but I hated to break with him, an old friend, for matters that seemed to be more his misfortune than intention. Tell Sammy and George to continue their love and when reason begins to hold its empire in their little bosoms, it will teach them they can be friends without fighting.

I have slipped a little way out of camp, have been here 4 or 5 days, don't know what minute we march, or where to. We are all so ill.

Please to give my respectful compliments to your revered father and Mother, your sisters and Brothers, Col. Eustace, his lady and family, my sister Randall, Mrs. Chilton, John Cooke, Mr. Hathaway, Capt. Randell Layton and all friends and believe me to be your obliged and aff. Brother,

John Chilton

I got a letter last week from Steerman which informed me of the welfare of our friends in the lower part of the County.
J.C.

Do pray tell your Brother Joe if he has an opportunity to bring a store of tobacco and ask my brother to have 2 or 3 dozen good twists made up for me this winter.

J.C.

Captain John Chilton to his Brother
Camp in Penn.
Aug. 17th^h, 1777

Dear Brother,

Yours by Mr. Morrison I with pleasure received last evening. I confess your prognostication of my ill success of rising in the Army was not without foundation, and has turned out according to your suspicion. It was confessed that they wished it in their power to give me a post my services and hardships entitled me to, but by so doing they would break that rule of rising by seniority of commissions. This I was told, had I been by I should have said that if due consideration had been observed in the appointing of officers in the army and disposing of posts a remonstrance from me would never have happened. I continue in favour with the Generals still, though old Genl. Stevens and myself had some very sharp words at Morristown.

The old saw of telling no tales out of school has as great a tendency to slavery as any one thing I know. A child may be brought up a slave, many parents wonder to see their sons turn out a silly lad and sometimes a cowardly, foolish, man, but never consider it is by cramping their genius at school where tyrants of masters leave such an impression on their tender minds that seldom they get over it. I am glad Joe is taken from that school and will not have to go to that master again on any account; for should the master promise to behave better and do so, the boy then in his turn will usurp – at any rate, don't let him go to the same master again. I should rather he should never know another letter than have the least taint of Scotch slavery, or any other kind, inculcated into him, and as I think him a generous boy and with a generous education will make a smart man.

I am sorry for your loss of poor Kate, she is really a great loss. I hope Jenny will get over her disposition. I have much rejoiced to get your letter, having heard that crops were poor in Virginia.

From 10th of July we have been continually marching, we have made a complete tour of the Jerseys, went into N. York state to a small town, Chester, where we staid one day. We next received marching orders. This was a forced march, from Chester N. York, to Brown's Ferry, Delaware River, is about 95 miles, this we marched in 4 days and had many impediments on the way. Horses dying on the way, shooeing of horses, mending wagons &c.

We went the Western road, saw several beautiful lakes, none above two miles long or 1 broad; the land is not so good here as the road we marched up. We staid all night in the Delaware post, had the misfortune to lose our baggage wagon in fording the River, tents and all. I had the luck to save my things as had Mr. Blackwell, Capt. Turner, and Mr. Mountjoy. They were all tied up in a tent and by reason of the bulk, the water could not easily soak through, so floated. From Delaware, we marched and encamped on the Schuylkill within 5 miles of Philadelphia, where we staid until the 8th of August, when we again marched, I expected to go to Ticonderoga but we are now stopped about 20 miles from Philadelphia near New Town. It was said in Camp yesterday that the enemy had landed in Egg Harbour in Jersey, and went on board again, but I find there is nothing to it.

To return to my disagreement with Genl. Stevens, some days ago, I had just gone up to drink our friends health in grog, the retreat beat, I told the Adjt. to step down while I paid, which I was doing when a sergeant and file of men came and informed me we must go to the Genl. I went down, very angry, making the poor Sergt. and his men keep their distance, when says the Genl. "Capt. Chilton, is it possible that you should be out of your duty". I told him "it was possible" but "could not submit that it then was, that the strictest discipline had been maintained, that all regulations allowed 5 minutes but that I had not taken 2, that I knew my duty and had done it and admitting I had made a slip thought it too trifling to be sent for in that way." He said he did not know we were officers, asked our pardon, asked us to drink grog, which we refused to do and went very angry away. The next day he called to me quite across a platoon of men to know "how I did" seemed sorry for what he had done, so I even thought it was best to be on good terms again.

But we have one gentleman in our Regmt. a Col. Wm. Heth who takes great things to himself. Heth does not lack sense but is imperious to the last degree. I was never tired of the Service till he joined the Regmt. I have a small notion of joining the Sea Service. If I could have the command of some clever little Brig or vessel, for I have no notions of Colonels, they are too overbearing to inferior officers and remarkably mean and cringing to their superiors. Heth has greatly the ascendancy over Marshall, which I could not have believed. Anything clever done in the Regmt. Heth takes credit for it, what is not well done is thrown on Marshall. Which will sink his credit as Heth's rises. We have parties as well as you. I am sorry for it, but can't help it. If Capt. William Blackwell were not out I should be almost tempted to quit the Service. His tent and mine adjoin so that we are always together when not on duty.

I pity Tom Keith's and Pickett's case. You have the consolation however that ill gotten power is seldom lasting. I saw a letter from Col. Lee to Col. Marshall and the answer which cleared the Col. of the imputations of your countrymen. Since then I have seen a Virginia paper and was glad that justice was at last done that gentleman.

I am of your opinion as to the injury the enlisting apprentices will do to the country. I think it would have been much better to have a draught and cut out those lazy fellows who are a pest to society.

I began this the 11th at this place —called the "Cross Roads". It is now the 21st of August. I expect to send it by John Bryan —We have orders to be ready for a march in the morning. Old Gray has just arrived in Camp, he was taken off the capes of Virginia some months ago and escaped from N. York last Sunday morning. Capt. Edward Travers who commanded the vessel is still a prisoner in N. York and treated extremely ill.

(The rest of this letter has been lost)

Appendix Two

The Diary of Captain John Chilton

Jan. 3d 1777 – 4 in the Morng.

The whole Army Marched from Trenton to Princeton, engaged a party of the enemy commanded by Major Leslie, defeated them. Leslie was Slain in this battle with other of his officers. As we were obliged to retreat at the beginning of the Battle the much lamented Genl. Mercer had his horse shot under him as he staid too much behind to conduct our retreat and was inhumanly murdered with Bayonets, &c. Majr. Fleming was killed in the engagement – Lieut. Yates had got a slight wound in the thigh which threw him into the hands of the enemy who immediately butchered him with the greatest Barbarity, we lost 12 or 14 in this engagement, 7 or 8 wounded slightly. The enemy had 30 or 40 killed and about as many more wounded. We took about 300 Prisoners, and should have had it in our power to take more but, as we had stolen our march from Trenton expected Gen. Grant on our backs from that place with 5 or 6000 Men. Our whole force did not amount to 2500, Pennsylvania Militia included, therefore were obliged to stop pursuit & gather our Men and march with expedition towards the Mountains, got to Somerset Courthouse that night, from Trenton 26 Miles

Next morng. early marched got to a small Town called Pluckimin where we got plenty of Beef Pork &c. which We had been starving for a day or two, not having time to draw and dress Victuals.

We staid here a day to refresh about 14 Miles from Somerset Court house to this place, from Pluckimin marched to Morris Town, where the 3d Virga. Regt. were stationed 4 or 5 days on side of a Mountain without Tents. Ground covered with snow.

From this uncomfortable place went to the House of Mr. Saml. Roberts and 2 Ms out Town where we staid a Fornight, then moved down to Morris Town where we staid till sometime in Febr. when we were ordered down to Hanover Township to be inoculated, we had the Small pox very lightly generally.

From Whippany or Hanover went to Chatham 7 Miles from Hanover which lies on the Pisiac, a smart River not navigable, here we staid until some time in April when we marched to Newark with an intent to cross over to Bergen where we heard 4 or 500 Tories were assembled but being disappointed in Boats did not cross, staid at Newark 2 or 3 day, then marched to the Matuchin Lines where we staid till 4th May when we were ordered to join the Grand Army at Middle Brook.

July 3d – His Excellency G. Washington with the Army marched from middle Brook to Morris Town by Whites Tavern where G. Lee was taken about 10 Miles from M. Brook within ½ Mile Lord Stirlings Seat to Morris Town from M. Brook 18 Ms. course E N 6 N.

Staid here till Saty 12th, when the whole Marched and encamped at the Western end of Pumpton Plains crossing Whippony at 4 Miles dist. going thro' a Town of same name in Hanover Township, took the Troy road & passed that Township, Crossed the Rockway River at 9 Ms Dist. which makes into Pisiac this river Runs Nearly S. W. till near its junction Pisiac & then runs nearly east. 3 Ms farther encamped which makes 16 Miles from Morris Town 17 from the encampmt. Sunday rain, on march here I lost my Journal from 15th Apl 77 to this date.

Monday (July) 14th – Genl. beat at day break crossed Beaver Dam Brook at ½ Miles dist. from thence to Paquonac River 7 Miles where there is a regular built fort, just below Mount Holly this fort is not proof against large Cannon – about 300 Yards farther crossed the long Pond River by some called Pumpton Rr. 4 Miles farther crossed a considerable Rr. in all 15 Miles.

Tuesday 15th – Marched up said Rr. 11 Miles to a place called the Clove here they call this Rr. Ramepo which winds thro' Large and Barren Mountains on the right a River not so large as the Ramepo empties into it from the Clove

18th July – we at 9 in forenoon Marched about 2 Miles back encamped in the Dutch Valley on sd Rr. Ramepo for the benefit of fresh & good Water – part of our encampment at the clove was in N. York State part in Jersey –

Sunday 20th – at Morng. Gun, the Tents were struck. Marched by the Clove, kept the course of Ramepo through as a road could not have been gotten any other way by reason of the Steep & rockiness of the Mountains there are very few houses for 16 Miles and they generally mean. the Valley being very narrow and for the most part so stony that no one can live: There are Deer (some say wild Goats) Vermin of various kinds & an abundance of Rattle Snakes. 'twas late before we encamped on the Western side of Haverstaw Mountn within 14 Miles New Windsor – the Mountns. to the left of encampmt Cheesequakes; from this place for near 30 Miles back the Country exhibits a very barren prospect the valley of Ramepo R being generally very narrow, about ½ Mile from this encampment the waters Run N. Easterly to North River. the Ramepo empties into Hackinsack being joined by several other Rivers the course Southerly – The waters emptying into

No. Rr is called Murderers Creek, some of the inhabitants thro' delicacy call it Murdenars;

21st & 22d – Staid here; about Mile and a half from hence on the Haverstraw Mount is a beautiful Lake near a Mile in Length & 400 Yds broad, clear and transparent said to be 30 or 40 feet deep abounding with various kinds fishes, near this Lake on the Mountain are Garden Gooseberries, Currans & Rasberries, the spontaneous growth of the place.

23d July – Marched at 9 in Morng 2 Miles to Smiths Tavern, from whence crossed Mountains a Westerly course 7 Miles to a place called Oxford, where we stopt to refresh. 4 Miles farther Chester, an insignificant place, like Oxford, neither of them Towns, passed thro' Chester and encamped.

24th – Lay by

25th – Early Marched from Chester 15 Miles on Way Breakfasted at one Wickhams before whose door is a pretty Lake 8 Miles farther encamped at a place called Warwiendah about a Mile & half in Jersey State where is a fine Spring.

26th – Tents struck at 3 in Morng. Marched 11 Miles by 9 Oclock breakfasted in a Meadow by a fine Spring, encamped at a place called Petitts 25 miles. On our March after breakfast went by Three Lakes all on right hand of road, a small River connects them the first is the smallest the Middle one near a Mile Long 400 Yards wide the Last or most southerly not quite ½ Mile Long 300 Yds wide. The Lakes about 4 Miles back of the encampment, the most Northerly – here is also a Furnace.

Before we Marched, Capt. Wallace, Capt. Powel, myself, Lt. Mercer, Lieut. Tebbs, Lieut. Baynham & Ensn. Payton were denied our Posts in Battalion, for this reason – there was a Genl. Order for every Officer to attend Roll Call at Retreat.

I had not seen my chest for near a week. I was consequently very dirty with a long beard. I had embraced this opporty. of Shaving & shifting and was about ½ shaved at beat. I saw the Men turn out and also saw Mr. Blackwell go to hear the Roll call. for this I was arrested – the other Gent. no doubt had their reasons or at least ought to have had, tho' to say truth this order has been too much neglected but to bring in those who had not neglected their duty indiscriminately with those who had, argues a New raised officer grasping a superiority and power. in 15 Minutes our Swords were ordered to be given us again, which all refused to receive but myself. I knew that Colo. Marshall had been urged to this place of strict tho' ill timed discipline, that he would act when it came to the pinch as it really turned out, and that it would end in a manner that would do neither party honour besides we were on a forced March where I knew we could have no trial until a battle should be fought as there was at that time the greatest prospect the report being that the enemy were some distance up the Delaware; and I was very averse to giving my command up to men of their choseg to command my Compy.

27th – By reason of rain the night past did not move till late this Morning—passed by a beautiful Lake in crossg the Mountain about 8 Mile Left hand side somewhat of an oval form about 350 & 300 Yds 3 Miles farther Hackitts Town (passed 2 Miles when we were ordered to sit down (in the Sun no water near) to refresh ourselves no victuals to eat as the **(word here indistinct)** of last night was so late that nothing could be cooked, no Waggons allowed to carry our Cooking Utensils, the soldiers were obliged to carry their Kettles pans &c. in their hands Clothes and provisions on their backs. As our March was a forced one & the Season extremely warm the victuals became putrid by sweat & heat – the Men badly off for Shoes, many being entirely barefoot and in our Regt. a too minute inspection was made into things relative to necessaries that the Men could not do without, which they were obliged to throw away. Encamped at Musconaconk Brooke 21 The Mountains having the same name of the Brooke the N. Eastern part of the same Ledge Mountains are called Pumpton these Mountains were on our Left from Smiths Tavern. near North Rr New York heights.

28th – Marched very early crossed the Masconeconk brooke 4 or 5 Miles below encampment. this days march as well as Yesterday we passed a deal barren Land. 17 Miles to PittsTown an inconsiderable place which we marched by 12 Oclock staid here till about 4 to refresh and draw provisions & moved to Quakers Town 2 Miles encamped.

29th – Marched by Sun, got 9 Miles & were ordered to Pitch tents where we staid that day a small Mile from road.

Next Morng. 30th – marched to Howels Ferry on Delaware opposite Brownes on the Pensylvania side 6 Miles.

31st – about 11 ordered to cross the River. had the misfortune of having our Waggon overset in fording the River this scheme of fording had like to have proved fatal to several soldiers, two were drowned a day or two before – we with difficulty saved ours. One horse was drowned the Waggon and chief of the Tents were lost. I lost my Tent but luckily the Bed clothes were wrapped up in Mr. Mountjoys Tent, and the bulk kept the water from soaking through so that they floated –encamped about 2 Miles from Rr our Regt. were obliged to take the woods for want Tents.

Augt. 1st – marched overtook Gen. Conways Brigade at 7 Miles dist. breakfasted at Thamony Bridge 2 Miles farther Cross road where are a few pretty good houses 2 Miles farther the Crooked Billet passed the Crooked Billet 2 Miles, encamped at forks of the Fall road.

2d. Augt. – Marched to German Town 9 Miles where we stopt about an Hr. Then marched 1 ½ miles & encamped near Schuylkill about 5 mile from Philadelphia. Here we staid till

Friday 8th Augt. – when we were Generally reviewed and ordered to March at 2 Oclock. We were told we should not march above 5 Ms. we passed the length of German Town which is 4 or 5 Miles and expected to halt a Mile or two out of Town. went very slowly. contd marching till 9 at night we supposed to get to some fine place but to our great mortification was put in a Stubble field as uneven as a Plough could make Ground and water half a Mile off & that very scarce and mean 11 Miles.

9th Augt. – at 9 Oclock moved a small mile for benefit Ground & water encamped at Sandy Brook.

Augt. 10th – Marched to Crooked billet 2 Miles farther encamped at cross Roads where we staid 'till

Saturday 23d Augt. – then Marched just before Sun got within 5 or 6 Miles Phila. encamped, recd. Orders for every Man to have clean clothes ready for the Morning, the Arms to be Furbished & bright.

24th – The whole was in motion by 4 in the Morning. marched in order a hard rain just as we entered down Water street and up Chestnutt Street crossed the Schuylkill on the floating bridge then made down the River to the Darby road and encamped at Darby a small Town. 12 Mile it is Navigable here for small Craft. in a creek of the Delaware

25th – Marched early in Morning at 8 Miles Dist. Chester a smart little but irregular built Town then Marcus Hook at about 3 Miles encamped within 2 ½ Miles Wilmington 15 Ms. The road runs within sight of the Delaware whose course is nearly West & sometimes a few points to the Southward. the Land here is not so rich as on the other side Delaware but well cultivated, fine Meadows and better Cattle. the inhabitants too, have not that griping importunate countenance as they have up to the N. Westward especially the ladies, whose features are more soft, and they also have sound teeth. We here saw however a specimen of the dissafection of some of the inhabitants in this County Newcastle. – Rain this eveng, as indeed there has been, particularly thro this Month, this whole Summer. Corn and every other vegetable exceedingly fine. The People of these States – Pensylvania Jerseys & N.York. throw 8 or 10 Grains of Indian corn in a hill and never thin it. they don't work their Corn as in Virga. and tho' 6 or 8 Stalks come up they do not give themselves the trouble of pulling the shoots or Suckers away. by tilling of a little Ground they have the Advantage of little Labour, a little Manure and beneficent crops. They don't work so hard as the Virginians. they make as much Money, but they do not live half so elegantly or even Plenteously. Were they to give their corn more distance and thin it I am certain they would find the benefit but they are prejudiced in their own way. they don't allow above 3 feet or 3 ½ feet for corn. The little Tobo. they pretend to raise they top at 18 & 20 Leaves –

Tuesday 26th – Marched to Wilmington then took a road which Lead N. Westwd. and marched 2 Miles, encamped called camp near Wilmington. The enemy it is said have Landed and about 3000 last night took Possession of Iron hill, which is about 12 Miles from the place of their Landing and about 12 Ms. from us. His Excellency the Genl. has gone done to observe their position. Our Light horse took 2 of theirs; Lay at this camp 1 day an abundance of rain fell the last night and part of this Morng. (27th.)

28th – Genls. Green & Stephens Divisions Marched, returning to Brandywine, a small Town chiefly consisting in Mills &

Taverns 8 or 10 Mills being within 100 Yards of each other a
Navigable Creek runs up to the Mills the Water is brought in
canals from Brandywine Creek. there appears to be a smart
fall of waters just above the Mills about ½ Mile farther on the
South side of a gradual hill in Wilmington the front or Road
Street is regular enough: paved within rails the town is built
irregularly towards the West – they have a Market house a
Navigable creek makes to the Southwd of the Town (called
Christeen) 4 Ms farther an inconsiderable Town, Newport.
Here we saw some fine Girls not much unlike our first Virga.
Nymphs. This day I was Capt. of Rare Guard and stopt about
a Mile out. About 12 Oclock, Colo. Hollingsworth came by
us wounded in the cheek or neck; about 2, the Commisary's
Waggons returned by them & some with them heard that the
Ministerials were advancing within a few Miles of us (scary
creatures) said there were 16,000 which our Soldiers as much
believed as they believe as they believe George III and his
corrupt Ministry have a right to tax America – here we staid
'till 4 – Marched not more than a Mile, when we stopt till after
sunset, when we were relieved and joined the regt. lay in the
woods without Pitching Tents.

29th – Moved about half Mile pitched Tents to dry them at 4
in afternoon moved about 3 Miles to the Eastward pitched
Tents and staid this night Within these three days near 50
Prisoners have been brought in. The enemy seem to be bold
but very imprudent. should they continue to act as they have
done a few Months will give them into our hands without
fighting. We have better than 1000 Men near them who will I
expect give a good account of those bloodsuckers, who shall
be guilty of the temerity of Leaving their Camp for the
atrocious crime of robbery, rapine & murder.—

30th Augt. – Officer of the day. Staid here this day & night

Sunday 31st. – continued still in Camp this Camp was in Christeen Hundred. our scouters took 7 Ministerials & one deserted to us. Colo Heath who was with the advanced detachment came in for provisions &c.

Monday Septr 1st – a detachmt was ordered out this eveng but did not go by reason of Rain till Tuesday Morg.

2d Septr – Capt. Ashby, Lt. White & Lt. V. Peyton went with the detachment. Colo Heth did not sett out 'til this Morng, this a close cloudy morng.

3d Septr. – The enemy advanced as high as the red Lion they were met by our advanced party under Colo. Crawford – the engagement was pretty hot. several on each side were wounded and some slain strong reinforcements were sent which obliged our Men to give Ground. the enemy returned. Our Division (Genl. Stephen's) went to our alarm posts staid a few Hours and returned to camp pitched our Tents & slept heartily.

4th Septr. – staid in camp at Night I was on Guard at a Bridge Red Clay Creek about Mile & half off and near our alarm post with 2 Subs. 2 Serjeants 2 Corpls. & 40 privates a peaceable Gd this night –Lieut. Davis of the Pensylvania Troops & Ensn. Westfall both of Scotts Brigade were with me early this Morning came down about 600 Men Viz. 200 first with the Qr. Masters bearing entrenching Tools. Colo. Febigar with 200 & Colo Willis with 200 they were followed by Waggons loaded with axes with which they felled trees plashing them to form a line by.---about 2 in afternoon Majr. Genl. Sullivans Division came down & took possession of the Lines we had been Plashing. It consists of between 2 & 3000 effective Men. At night was relieved by Capt. Stephen Ashby

6th Septr. – G. Stephens Division March by Sun, about a Mile Encamped at Camp near Newpt. Staid here this night as we expected the enemy would be in motion early in the Morning of Sunday

7th – every necessary order was given to be in readiness.—the deserters from the enemy inform that on Saturday Morng they drew 5 days provisions which were to serve them to Philadela. or Wilmington at least. that their Tents and heavy Baggage were sent back to their Ships.

Monday 8th Septr. – the enemy approached as near as Newark. We all lay at our alarm posts.

Tuesday 9th at 2 in the morning we had orders to march took the road from Newport to Wilmington 2 Miles then turned to almost North about 2 Ms more we then marched West course 10 Miles S.W. & crossed Brandywine Creek and encamped on the heights of the Creek.

Bibliography

Alcock, John. Fauquier Families 1759-1799: Comprehensive
Indexed Abstracts of Tax & Tithable Lists, Marriage Bonds
and Minute, Deed, and Will Books. Athen, GA: Iberian
Publishing, 1994.

Anderson, Enoch. "Personal Recollections of Captain Enoch
Anderson, an officer of the Delaware Regiments in the
Revolutionary War", Historical and Biographical Papers of
The Historical Society of Delaware. vol. 2, no. 16, 1896.

Beale, Robert. "Revolutionary Experiences of Major Robert
Beale", Northern Neck of Virginia Historical Magazine.
December 6, 1956.

Boatner, Mark Mayo, Encyclopedia of the American
Revolution. New York: D. McKay Co., 1966.

Boyle, Joseph Lee. Writings from the Valley Forge
Encampment of the Continental Army: December 19,
1777 June 19, 1778, Vol. 1-2. Bowie, MD: Heritage
Books, 2001.

Buck, Dee Ann. Abstracts of Fauquier County, Virginia:
Wills, Inventories, & Accounts 1759-1799. 1998

Carrington, Henry B. Battles of the American Revolution
1775-1781. New York: A. S. Barnes & Co., 1877.

Commager, Henry Steele and Morris, Richard B., eds. The
Spirit of 'Seventy-Six. New York: Bobbs-Merrill, 1973.

Dann, John C. The Revolution Remembered: Eyewitness Accounts of the War Independence. Chicago: University of Chicago Press, 1980.

Dwyer, William. The Day Is Ours! : An Inside View of the Battles of Trenton and Princeton, November 1776 – January 1777. New Brunswick, New Jersey : Rutger University Press, 1983.

Ewald, Johann. Diary of the American War, A Hessian Journal, Captain Johann Ewald, Field Jaeger Corps. New Haven and London: Yale University Press, 1979. (Translated and edited by Joseph Tustin)

Gott, John K. Abstracts of Fauquier County Virginia, Wills, Inventories & Accounts: 1759-1800. 1976

Gott, John K. Fauquier County, Virginia Guardian Bonds: 1759-1871. Bowie, MD: Heritage Books, 1990

Fitzpatrick, John C, (ed.). The Writings of George Washington from the Original Manuscript Sources, 1745-1799. (Accessed Online at the Library of Congress under The George Washington Papers)

Fleming, Thomas. 1776: Year of Illusion. New York: W.W. Norton, 1975.

Force, Peter, ed. American Archives: 5th Series. 3 vol. Washington D.C.: U.S. Congress, 1848-1853.

Graham, Daniel. Life of General Daniel Morgan of the Virginia Line of the Army of the United Stated. 1856 (Reprint, 1993).

Goodwin, Mary. <u>Clothing and Accoutrements of the Officers and Soldiers of the Virginia Forces : 1775-1780</u>. Unpublished, 1962.

Haller, Stephen E. <u>William Washington, Cavalryman of the Revolution</u>. Bowie, MD: Heritage Books, 2001.

Hening, William. <u>The Statutes at Large being a collection of all the Laws of Virginia from the first session of the Legislature. Vol. 9</u>. 1821.

Johnston, Henry P. <u>The Battle Of Harlem Heights</u>. London : Macmillian, 1897.

Johnston, Henry P. <u>The Campaign of 1776 around New York and Brooklyn</u>. Brooklyn: Long Island Historical Society, 1878.

Katcher, Philip. "They Behaved Like Soldiers: The Third Virginia Regiment at Harlem Heights", <u>Virginia Cavalcade.</u>Vol. 26, No. 2, Autumn 1976.

Ketchum, Richard M. <u>The Winter Soldiers : The Battles for Trenton and Princeton</u>. New York : Henry Holt & Co., 1973.

King, Estelle Stewart. <u>Abstract of Wills, Administrations and Marriages of Fauquier County Virginia 1759-1800</u>. Baltimore: Genealogical Publishing Co., 1980.

Lee, Charles. <u>The Lee Papers vol. 1-2</u>. New York: Collections of the New York Historical Society, 1871.

Lee, Henry. <u>The Revolutionary War Memoirs of General Henry Lee</u>. New York: Da Capo Press, 1970, Originally Published in 1812.

Lesser, Charles H. (ed.). The Sinews of Independence: Monthly Strength Reports of the Continental Army. Chicago: University of Chicago Press, 1976.

Marshall, John. The Life of George Washington. Vol.2. Fredericksburg, VA: The Citizens' Guild of Washington's Boyhood Home, 1926.

Martin, Joseph Plum. Private Yankee Doodle. Edited by George F. Scheer. New York: Little, Brown, 1962.

McGuire, Thomas. The Surprise of Germantown: October 4th, 1777. Cliveden of the National Trust for Historic Preservation, 1994.

McIlwaine, H. R. ed. Journals of the Council of the State of Virginia. 3 vol. Richmond: Virginia State Library, 1926.

McMichael, James. "The Diary of Lt. James McMichael, of the Pennsylvania Line 1776-1778," The Pennsylvania Magazine of History and Biography. Vol. 16, No. 2, 1892.

Moore, Frank. Diary of the American Revolution, from Newspapers and Original Documents. 2 vols. New York: Charles Schibner, 1860. Reprint. New York: New York Times & Arno Press, 1969.

Mowday, Bruce E. September 11, 1777, Washington's Defeat at Brandywine Dooms Philadelphia. Shippensburg, PA: White Mane Books, 2002.

Peale, Charles Willson. "Journal by Charles Willson Peale", Dec. 4, 1776-Jan. 20, 1777." Pennsylvania Magazine of History and Biography. 38, 1914.

Peters, Joan W. The Tax Man Cometh: Land & Property in
Colonial Fauquier County, Virginia 1759-1782.
Westminster, MD: Willow Bend Books, 1999

Posey, John Thornton. General Thomas Posey: Son of the
American Revolution. East Lansing, MI: Michigan State
Univ., 1992

Powell, Robert. "David Griffith to Major Levin Powell, May
28, 1777" Biographical Sketch of Col. Levin Powell,
1737 – 1810: Including his Correspondence during the
Revolutionary War. Alexandria. Virginia: G.H. Ramey &
Son, 1877.

Reed, John F. Campaign to Valley Forge: July 1, 1777 –
December 19, 1777. Philadelphia: University of
Pennsylvania Press, 1965.

Rowland, Kate Mason. The Life and Correspondence of
George Mason. New York: Russell & Russell, 1964.

Russell, T. Tripplett and John K. Gott. Fauquier County in
the Revolution. Westminster, MD : Willow Bend Books,
1988.

Saffell, W.T.R. Records of the Revolutionary War.
Baltimore: MD, 1894.

Sanchez-Saavedra, E. M. "All Fine Fellows and Well
Armed", Virginia Cavalcade. Vol. 24, No. 1, Summer
1974.

Sanchez-Saavedra, E. M. A Guide to Virginia Military
Organizations in the American Revolution : 1774 – 1787.
Richmond : Virginia State Library, 1978.

Scheer, George F., and Hugh F. Rankin. Rebels & Redcoats: The American Revolution through the Eyes of Those Who Fought and Lived It. New York: Da Capo Press, 1987.

Scribner, Robert L. and Tarter, Brent (comps). Revolutionary Virginia: The Road to Independence. volumes 1 thru 7. Charlottesville: University Press of Virginia, 1978.

Selby, John E. The Revolution in Virginia : 1775-1783. New York : Holt Inc., 1996.

Sellers, John R. The Virginia Continental Line. Williamsburg: The Virginia Bicentennial Commission, 1978.

Simcoe, Lt. Col. John. Simcoe's Military Jouirnal: A History of the Operations of a Partisan Corps Called the Queen's Rangers, Commanded by Lieut. Col. J. G. Simcoe, During the War of Revolution. New York: New York Times and Arno Press, 1968.

Slaughter, Philip. A History of St. Mark's Parish : Culpeper County Virginia. 1877.

Smith, Jean Edward. John Marshall : Definer of a Nation. New York : Holt Inc., 1996.

Smith, Samuel. The Battle of Brandywine. Monmouth Beach, NJ: Philip Freneau Press, 1976.

Smith, Samual S. The Battle of Trenton. Monmouth Beach, NJ: Philip Freneau Press, 1965

Stryker, William. <u>The Battles of Trenton and Princeton</u>. Republished by The Old Barracks Assoc., Trenton NJ: 2001, Originally published in 1898.

Symonds, Craig L. <u>A Battlefield ATLAS of the American Revolution</u>. The Nautical & Aviation Publishing Co. of America Inc., 1986.

Thacher, James. <u>A Military Journal during the American Revolutionary War</u>. Hartford: CT, S. Andrus and Son, 1854. Reprint, New York: Arno Press, 1969.

Townsend, Joseph . "Some Account of the British Army under the Command of General Howe, and of the Battle of Brandywine", <u>Eyewitness Accounts of the American Revolution.</u> New York, Arno Press, 1969

Tyler, Lyon, ed. "The Old Virginia Line in the Middle States During the American Revolution", <u>Tyler's Quarterly Historical and Genealogical Magazine, vol. 12</u>. Richmond, VA: Richmond Press, Inc., Printer, 1931 (Includes: The Diary and Letters of Captain John Chilton)

<u>Virginia Gazette</u>. October 3, 1777, Williamsburg, Printed by Dixon & Hunter.

Ward, Christopher. <u>The Delaware Continentals, 1776-1783</u>. Wilmington, DE: History Society of Delaware, 1941.

Ward, Harry M. Duty, Honor, or Country : General George <u>Weedon and the American Revolution</u>. Philadelphia : American Philosophical Society, 1979.

Wright, Robert K. <u>The Continental Army</u>. Washington, D.C. Center of Military History: United States Army, 1989.

Wrike, Peter Jennings. The Governor's Island: Gwynn's Island, Virginia, During the Revolution. Gwynn, VA: The Gwynn's Island Museum, 1993.

Index

ABOUT THE AUTHOR

MICHAEL CECERE SR. is the proud father of two incredible children, Jenny and Michael Jr., and a grateful husband to Susan Cecere. He teaches American History at Robert E. Lee High School in Fairfax County, Virginia and is entering his 13th year as a public school teacher. He also teaches American History and American Government (part time) at Northern Virginia Community College. He holds a Master of Arts degree in History and another in Political Science. An avid Revolutionary and Civil War re-enactor, he participates in numerous living history events and demonstrations throughout the year. He contributes articles to the Brigade of the American Revolution, as well as to the newsletters of his re-enacting units, the 3rd and 7th Virginia Regiments. He is also the editor of the 7th Virginia's newsletter. Currently he is conducting research on another forgotten patriot, Lt. Col. Charles Porterfield of Frederick County, Virginia.